Your First Year in Sales

Available from
YOUR FIRST YEAR Series:

Your First Year As an Elementary School Teacher
Your First Year As a High School Teacher
Your First Year As a Nurse
Your First Year in Real Estate
Your First Year in Sales

Your First Year in

Sales

*Making the Transition from Total
Novice to Successful Professional*

TIM CONNOR, CSP

 THREE RIVERS PRESS
NEW YORK

Published by Three Rivers Press, New York, New York.
Member of the Crown Publishing Group, a division of Random House, Inc.
www.crownpublishing.com

THREE RIVERS PRESS and the Tugboat design are registered trademarks of Random House, Inc.

Originally published by Prima Publishing, Roseville, California, in 2001.

All products mentioned in this book are trademarks of their respective companies.

Printed in the United States of America

Library of Congress Cataloging-in-Publication Data

Connor, Tim.
    Your first year in sales : making the transition from total novice to successful professional / Tim Connor.
        p. cm. — (Your first year)
    Includes index.
    1. Selling. I. Title. II. Your first year series.

HF5438.25 .C6553 2001
658.85—dc21

2001021656

ISBN 0-7615-3411-3

10 9 8 7 6 5
First Edition

To Dad. Your example, support, inspiration, and insight stand as a beacon in my life as I share my lessons with the world.

Contents

Acknowledgments ————————————————

There are hundreds of people who have touched my life and contributed to my knowledge, including clients, audience members, peers, and friends. Special mention goes to those who stand out in my life and have always been there for me as I grew in wisdom and maturity: my fellow members of Master Speakers International, Tom Winninger, Charlie "Tremendous" Jones, and especially my wife, Jann, who is a constant source of encouragement and support.

Introduction _____

In sales as in life, sometimes it is best to get right to the point. Thus, I will keep my introduction short and allow us to get to the great material that follows.

The average cost of a sales call today is over $400—regardless of whether you close the sale or not. Can you imagine the yearly investment for your company, even if it has only twenty-five salespeople making an average of four calls a day? That's eight million dollars a year! And that doesn't include any extra compensation such as bonuses or commissions, special training, attending sales meetings, and anything and everything else.

Now I ask you, why should a company invest that much of its income on a sales force that is less than professional, poorly trained, or generally has a negative attitude? I don't have an answer to that one, but I can tell you that if sooner or later they don't recoup that investment, you will be looking for a new employer.

During my twenty-five-year sales training career, I have done some research on the amount of time salespeople spend actually selling. What I have learned is that the average salesperson spends less than 10 to 20 percent of total work time selling and more than 80 percent doing everything else, like traveling, attending meetings, managing paperwork, servicing customers, handling after-sales problems, and the many other tasks that come with being in sales. Can you imagine for a moment, a company paying salespeople over fifty thousand dollars a year to do paperwork? For windshield time? For after-sales service? Don't fool yourself. You are paid to sell—period. Yes, your position has other requirements; but in the end, how much you have sold will determine your income, status, success, and lifestyle.

There are numerous advantages to a career in sales, and I will cover many of these in the first chapter. But for now I'll assume that you are reading this book because you want to succeed—now—in your new career. Your sales success—immediate and ongoing—will be a function of many skills and attitudes. In the pages that follow, you will learn the essentials as well as what will put you over the top and turn you into a sales leader.

First, you need to answer a serious question: Why have you selected a career in sales? Did it happen by accident? Did you assume that since you couldn't make it in another career that you could always sell for a living? Was it for the money? Freedom? Glamour? Or something else? Your honest answer to this question, before you settle into a career in selling, may well determine your success. Many people who could have done really well in sales quit because they never answered this question. They had no clear expectation of what they wanted to get out of sales.

Second, ask yourself what you are willing to give up to enjoy the success you say you want. Earning success takes sacrifice. That's why you *earn* success.

And finally, ask yourself what motivates you to continue—anything—when life throws you a curve. There will be curves in this profession, like any other, and the more you have thought about how you will deal with them the better prepared you will be to overcome them when you encounter unexpected obstacles.

I have been in sales for forty years. Obviously, I am doing something right, or I wouldn't have lasted this long. I can tell you that a successful sales career is worth the effort, price, commitment, and time. Many people want to take the easy road. The easy road goes nowhere; trust me. Sooner or later, your resolve, goals, commitment, will, and desire will be tested. Whether you pass the test is up to you and no one else. Be prepared to be tested over and over. If you have a weak spirit, shallow resolve, and tendency to quit or give up early, commit yourself to toughening up and take the appropriate steps to do so or save yourself the trouble. While it may sound strange to discourage you before you even begin, my purpose in writing this book is to contribute to your success and the satisfaction of your customers, *not* to give excuses to the weakhearted.

I love this profession. It has given me the ability to live as I want. It can give that to you, too. But you will have to do the work. You will have to study, practice, learn, try, fail, and get up again and again. And if you do, you will look back with pride, satisfaction, gratitude, and a smile.

That's it. Now let's get to it!

It's Your Move

Welcome to the exciting profession of sales. You deserve to be congratulated for choosing sales and thus making the decision to determine your destiny, lifestyle, and personal freedom. Approached with the proper attitude, skills, determination, and knowledge, the field of sales can be an exciting career. Reading this book is the perfect start to that career.

I have been selling for more than forty years and teaching people to sell for more than twenty-five. I have seen and taught people of both genders and from all backgrounds, nationalities, education levels, and races.

Whether you succeed has absolutely nothing to do with any of those characteristics. Your sole need is the will to succeed; commitment to excellence; effort; willingness to learn, grow, and change;

your desire to serve others; persistence in difficult times and situations; and your staying power.

Sales is not an easy profession, but the harder you work, the greater your rewards. The sales profession is full of obstacles—difficult people, countless challenges, and numerous dead ends. But it is also the source of a lot of fun, a great deal of satisfaction, personal security, excitement, tremendous earning potential, and daily opportunities to meet wonderful people from different walks of life.

I'll let you in on a secret: I was fired from my first sales position more than thirty-five years ago. But with time, patience, a lot of effort and study, years later I sold *that same company* some sales training. Yes! Cha ching. All it took was belief in myself, persistence, and a lot of hard work. Believe me when I say it was well worth it.

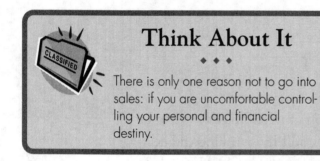

Think About It

◆ ◆ ◆

There is only one reason not to go into sales: if you are uncomfortable controlling your personal and financial destiny.

Throughout this book are the hints, tips, secrets, and rules for success. Together, they create our formula that will lead you to succeed during your first year as a salesperson. It will describe in detail the attitudes you need to develop, the skills you must master, and the philosophy you should adopt.

Our Own Quick Start

This profession will change you as well as challenge you to grow personally and professionally. You are the only one who can determine your success and what you give to and take from your sales career as it unfolds in the months and years ahead.

For me, getting into this wonderful profession was one of the best decisions I ever made. I have met all of my friends during the course of this career. Everything I have learned was because of this profession. And all of the satisfaction I have gained and any contribution I have made to society was made possible by my occupation as a salesperson. My goal here is give you everything you need to be able to look back years from now and say the same things.

What Is a Professional Salesperson?

For years I have heard people use the word "professional," especially when they are refer to salespeople. How would you define a professional? I have been asking my audiences for years to describe a sales professional. The consensus is that a professional salesperson is:

- Well-groomed.
- Punctual.
- Well dressed.
- Honest.
- Knowledgeable.

The Quick-Start Concept

In sports, there is a concept called the "quick-start concept." It means that the first team to score in any game has a greater chance of winning the game than does its opponent. The same can be said for sales, where the quick-start concept means you must:

- Come out of the gate each year on January 1 at a dead run.
- Begin each new week with a good sale.
- Start each month with a positive outlook and expectations.
- Start the day early with a positive plan for success.
- Jump-start your new career and quickly move into the fast lane.

This book will give you the tools to do just that. If you read this book, study it, live it, and breathe it, I guarantee that you will be ahead of the pack before you've even finished your first year as a salesperson. You will set sales records, position yourself for long-term success, and immediately earn the respect of your customers, peers, friends, and supervisor.

- Positive with a good attitude.
- Courteous and doesn't bad-mouth the competition.
- Customer focused.
- Dependable.
- Caring.
- Creative problem solver.
- Good at sales follow-up.

This list could go on for several pages. Again, I ask you, how would you define a professional? To me, being a professional is not what you sell, but how you sell. Let me explain. Some people selling

Salespeople Are Not Becoming Obsolete

Will the continuous advances in technology replace the profession of selling in the foreseeable future? I am not a fortune-teller or a mystic, but I do believe that we will see dramatic changes in the roles salespeople play within their organizations and the economy in general. During the next several years, even the next few decades, we will see dramatic and all-encompassing change in every industry, field, and profession. No one will go untouched by the swath that will cut across every age group and discipline.

We are rapidly becoming a society that no longer talks to each other face-to-face. We communicate by fax machine, computer, e-mail, answering machines, and voice mail. We are losing the human touch. But as salespeople, we bridge the gap between this impersonal electronic world and our human customers—one of several reasons why the sales profession is alive and well and will continue to play a vital role in a growing economy for years. Salespeople are charged with any or all of the following:

- They present new ideas, concepts, products, and services to present and potential clients.
- They assess the marketplace and gauge customer satisfaction levels and perceptions, general market attitudes, competitors' strengths and weaknesses, and consumer interest trends.

high-priced and highly regarded products are far from professional. I have met some pretty sleazy salespeople selling very expensive products and services, and I have had the pleasure of doing business with some really great people selling low-price consumables.

So, selling is not what you sell, but how you sell what you sell. Ask yourself: How am I doing when it comes to being a professional? How do you want your clients or customers to think of you? How do you want your competitors to think about you? How do you want the marketplace to view your activity? Don't wait for the results to come in from these sources. Ask yourself and adapt your style and attitude to match your desired result.

- They witness and report on the emergence of grass-root market shifts, trends, and interests.
- They soothe ruffled egos of disappointed, frustrated, and angry customers.
- They provide bottom-up feedback to the management of their organization on any number of opportunities, problems, and issues.
- They are the front line of attack for any number of corporate marketing strategies and programs.
- They work the trade show booths (a grueling task, if you have never done it) in thousands of trade shows each year.
- They are on the lookout for new product or service opportunities that a "corporate" person would never see.
- They are ambassadors for management, building positive ongoing relationships that can increase business and profits.

I challenge you to find a computer, fax machine, software program, customer service representative, or marketing person who can do all of this with the: courage of a mountain climber; patience of Job; willingness to sacrifice of a humanitarian; energy of a two-year-old; creativity of Frank Lloyd Wright; dedication of a mother; wisdom of Confucius; enthusiasm of a cheerleader; commitment of an Olympic athlete; and the persistence of a toddler trying to reach the cookie jar. The role of the sales professional will continue to shift and change, but the fundamental mission will remain intact.

Attitudes for Sales Success

The way you prepare for each day, each sale, and how you respond to your successes and failures will ultimately determine just how enjoyable and lucrative your career in sales will be. Let's touch on a few of the critical attitudes and behaviors you must develop if you are to succeed.

Persistence. You must have persistence. More often than not, people will put off saying yes to your presentation and/or demonstration. The key is knowing how to discover the prospect's critical sense of urgency and when the best times to persevere with that potential customer are. Equally important is the ability to not be discouraged when you are rejected or unsuccessful.

Resilience. People will say "no," with that being their final answer. Whether you have the fortitude to march on, even with such rejections, will play a large part in determining your success.

Interest in Self-Improvement. Be willing to learn new skills and attitudes. There is *always* something new you can learn and attitudes you can acquire. Those who stay knowledgeable about new trends and corporate thinking remain on top of the sales leaderboard.

Think About It

♦ ♦ ♦

Your ability to direct and guide a prospect's thinking is directly related to your ability to control your own thoughts.

Confident Yet Modest. Keep your ego in check. Today may have been great; tomorrow could be just the opposite. Keep a level head. The ups and downs of sales can be frequent, and the higher you let your ego float, the harder and farther can fall.

Flexibility. The ability to work effectively in a less-than-ideal business environment is essential. No company is perfect. Few sales situations are ideal. The key is to be able to take a difficult situation or set of circumstances and turn them into a positive outcome. For example: I can recall, in my second sales position, my workspace was about five square feet with a school-sized desk to work from. The telephone was on a window shelf behind me. Not ideal circumstances by any stretch of anyone's imagination. But, I had to sell regardless of my environment. I quickly figured out that if I let the circumstances dictate my attitude, I was in big trouble. So, I simply looked at it as only a temporary situation. I kept telling myself that if I could be successful under those circumstances, I could sell anywhere, anytime.

Professionalism. Be adept at cultivating positive working relationships—even with those who can be difficult to work with. Not everyone has to be your best friend. Be open to developing a positive business relationship with *anyone*. Business is business, friendship is friendship—but here, business is the name of this game.

Motivation. Keep yourself motivated. Again, business is business. No matter what distractions you have in your personal life or your life outside of work, you must be able to put on your game face every day and get the job done.

Self-Control. Control your attitudes and emotions. Keeping your attitudes and emotions at the appropriate level for the situation is a must. Knowing when and how to react will help you enormously in your career.

Each of these attitudes and behaviors is something you must develop to ensure your success.

What to Expect

Selling is fun and rewarding. You help people solve problems, overcome challenges, improve their sales or results, or maybe help them sleep better at night because of your creative solutions. The average professional salesperson keeps at least thirty other people employed in our economy. That, my friend, is a worthy professional accomplishment. This success, however, does not come cheap. You'll face hurdles, challenges, problems, risks, and potential failures that will frustrate you. And there are always many other things to turn your attention to if the frustration gets the best of you. However, you'll experience an overflowing feeling of satisfaction with each obstacle cleared. If you prepare to experience all of the following, then you will be better prepared to endure the challenging times and manage the prosperous periods.

The average professional salesperson keeps at least thirty other people employed in our economy.

Here's what you can expect, good and bad:

- Long days.
- A sense of satisfaction.
- Early-morning risings.
- Controlling your destiny.
- Late nights.
- Lots of new friends.
- Evening appointments.
- Opportunities for personal growth.
- Time away from friends and family.
- A chance to make more money than you ever dreamed possible.
- Stress, pressure, and deadlines.
- The ability to contribute to the success of others.

- Upset customers.
- To be paid what you are worth.
- Demanding bosses.
- Travel.
- Unethical competitors.

If you approach your new career with a heads-up attitude, you will certainly enjoy your share of the good times. Inevitably, though, some of the negative elements will also creep into your career. Just remember that it is natural to want to quit something when it is new and difficult. It is human nature to want everything to be easy. Problem is, if everything was easy, you wouldn't get the same sense of satisfaction and joy. Struggle, once overcome, is the source of all of our good feelings about ourselves. No challenge? Well, sure, you may get the prize, but I guarantee you won't enjoy it as much. This comes from someone who has failed far more often than he has ever succeeded. The book you are now reading is the result of more than twenty years of trying to convince hundreds of publishers that I had something valuable say.

I am not a pessimist. I am not a realist. I have found there is no value in anything less than pure optimism. I grew up failing. Most of us endure many, many failures over our lifetimes. I'll just say that sooner or later, your worth will be tested, not by your successes but by your failures. There is nothing wrong with wanting to quit. Just don't do it. Give yourself the benefit of the doubt when life throws you curves. The light is always at the end of the tunnel, but you have to keep on driving to reach it. If you can both weather these difficulties and not let success make you arrogant, believe me, the journey will be well worth it.

> *The light is always at the end of the tunnel, but you have to keep on driving to reach it.*

Traps to Avoid

New salespeople are vulnerable to falling into any number of traps or going in directions that lead to dead ends. Some of these may seem insignificant at first, but do not be lulled into a false sense of security. Remember that you are in the formative months of a new profession and forming habits that will be with you for years—whether good or bad ones. Don't risk it. The price of failure is far too high. Your customers will set some of these traps; others may be set by your fellow salespeople or support staff. Even your supervisor may set you some traps.

Remember that you are in the formative months of a new profession and forming habits that will be with you for years—whether good or bad ones.

One of the biggest traps is developing the habit of comparing yourself and your success to other salespeople who are either on your sales team or are your competitors. Your success is not measured by a comparison to anyone. It is only measured by the relationship between what you are doing and what you could be doing.

I remember in my first sales position, I was discouraged because I was always on the bottom of the list of salespeople at the end of the month when the results were tallied. I became anxious, frustrated, and began to focus on not doing things wrong rather than on doing them right, or paying attention to what I was learning or how I was progressing. Avoid this trap.

Years later, when I was a veteran, one of my fellow salespeople who was doing better than I kept trying to manipulate me into believing that even though I was doing well, I would never really hit the big time in sales. Fortunately, I had enough belief in myself that his words had no long-term negative impact on me.

The traps are out there. Keep your eyes out for them.

What You Need to Learn

Any new career requires you to develop new skills, attitudes, and knowledge of the job itself.

You will need time, patience, an open mind, a willingness to learn, flexibility, and the ability to let go of the old baggage from your previous career position. This old baggage can take the form of previous slights, failures, relationship challenges, company polices or procedures that you didn't like or agree with, and numerous other issues. You'll also have to leave behind any expectations that are not based in a solid foundation of reality.

Sales is not like any other career. To be successful in sales requires a unique set of people skills, sales techniques, relationship skills, attitude management skills, and effective time and territory management. You have a great deal to learn. Be patient with yourself as you develop these new habits, attitudes, and techniques. This does not mean that you should not throw yourself into your new position with everything you have. It only implies that learning new skills and techniques requires time. You must learn how to:

- Manage and overcome the fear of rejection.
- Cultivate positive relationships with support staff.
- Meet the expectations of your supervisor.
- Balance your time between selling, learning, and personal and family time.
- Determine which prospects are worthy of your time.
- Keep yourself motivated when things go wrong.
- Keep personal challenges, issues, and negatives out of your mind while selling.
- Not to beat yourself to a pulp when things go wrong.

Patience is your biggest virtue while you are learning your new trade. With patience, you will learn faster and enjoy the ride toward success. Without patience, you will have a tough time learning the right way to do anything. Be aggressive, but also thoughtful, as you move along.

One Word—*Ask*—Is All It Takes

Ask, Ask, Ask

You must ask your customers:

- For the order (the obvious one).
- For referrals, each and every time.
- For letters of testimony from every contact.
- Questions, a lot of them, and keep asking them.
- If you may use them as a reference (this can get you more business).
- Why they did business with you. You need to know.
- Why they *didn't* do business with you (every lost sale).
- For the right to use third-party influence.
- How you can best service them.
- There are many more. In fact, you should constantly be adding and updating your list of questions as you gain experience. You can then tailor it to your particular position as you start to understand what it takes to be successful.

This three-letter word is at the root of more failure and success in sales than any other I know. People who consistently succeed in sales, whatever success means to them, do so because they ask for what they want. Salespeople who fail tend to do so because they fail to either know what they want or how to ask for it. If you ask the right people the right questions and learn everything you can, you will undoubtedly reap the benefits in many areas of your career. Figure 1 shows you how.

Years ago I made a cold call on the president of a Fortune 500 company. I'll never forget it. He actually saw me, and he taught me a valuable lesson. At the conclusion of the call, I asked him why he was willing to see me. He

Knowledge
▼
Belief
▼
Confidence
▼
Professionalism
▼
Improved Performance
▼
Income
▼
Satisfaction
▼
Success

Figure 1 Knowledge Is King

said, "No one has ever tried to see me as president without an appointment. I wanted to meet the person who had the guts to ask."

So don't miss another opportunity to achieve your dreams. Ask for what you want. There are only two outcomes when you do: You will get what you want or you won't. If you don't, you have lost nothing by asking. When in doubt—ask for it. Guess what? You might just get it. Failure is not about missing the mark, but not taking the first step.

Getting Organized

Getting organized means many things in the sales profession. You must mesh your materials, time, learning, territory, attitudes, and sales approaches. The foundation for becoming a highly organized person is an effective planning philosophy and strategy. Here are a few things to consider:

- Get up an hour earlier every day than you are accustomed to.

- Make an appointment with yourself every evening to plan your goals, activities, and objectives for the next day.
- Spend time preparing for each week and month.
- Schedule time every day for learning about your product, polishing your sales skills, and perfecting the strategies you use to manage your relationships.
- Develop positive work habits.
- Keep track of your time-wasters.
- Keep a time-and-activity log for your first three months on the job.
- Spend time each week with the seasoned salespeople and think of specific questions to ask them.
- Spend time regularly with your supervisor. Seek his or her response or feedback on specific questions.
- Develop the habit of asking lots of questions.
- Start a success journal. Keep track of your successes no matter how small you think they are.
- Set deadlines for yourself to master new skills or learn new information.
- Read, read, read. Keep your TV off for three months.
- Evaluate your time-use rituals, that is, reading the newspaper, watching TV, and the like.

Add to this list as you progress through your new career.

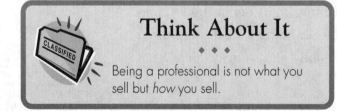

Think About It

♦ ♦ ♦

Being a professional is not what you sell but *how* you sell.

All of these things will pave the road for success—and you need them all. But what other traits do successful salespeople share?

Traits of Successful Salespeople

Successful salespeople have developed certain traits and attitudes that contribute to their success. I have been observing salespeople for a long time, and I can tell you that they all don't have all of the characteristics or abilities listed below. They are, however, able to master those traits that are critical for their particular product or service, organizational culture, and customer needs and expectations, as well as learn competitors' strengths and weaknesses. The following list is in no particular order, but it does give you an idea of the profile of success in the selling profession. Successful salespeople:

- Manage their attitudes from inside-out, not outside-in.
- Are on fire with passion and desire.
- Are a resource for their clients. They go the extra mile.
- Are excellent communicators.
- Are focused and concentrate on the task at hand.
- Are able to win the support of all inside support staff.
- Spend more time digesting information than giving it.
- Are masters at asking the right questions, in the right way and at the right time.
- Sell value not price. They know that, over time, this is the most important issue to the customer.
- Manage their resources of time, corporate resources, money, and people.
- Keep in touch with their clients and prospective clients regularly.
- Have quality service and customer loyalty as their primary goal.
- Honor their commitments.
- Give something back to their community and profession.

- Are everywhere at once. They network and understand the value of good contacts.
- Have lofty goals. They don't always reach them, but they aim for the stars.
- Promise a lot and deliver more.
- Understand the importance of knowledge of customers, competitors, and the marketplace.
- Give their word as their bond.
- Work hard and smart.
- Don't try only for the home runs. They know that if they just keep hitting singles consistently, sooner or later they will hit a home run.

A long list, I know, but if you want to separate yourself from the "also-rans" in this profession, mastering most of this list is vital. Even if takes you your entire career to do so, if you integrate these concepts into your selling behavior early, little by little, you can't help with time to become a superstar.

Why not measure yourself against this list and then, over time, ask your clients to do the same? You might find out some interesting and valuable information about how you are doing and progressing.

Creating a Trustworthy and Favorable Impression

There is an old saying—you never get a second chance to make a first impression. I don't really know whether it is true or not. Many old clichés have a way of hanging around for years, and no one ever questions them. Regardless, first impressions certainly are important, especially in business.

In your personal life, if you make a poor first impression on a new friend, it probably won't cost you your job or suddenly put you in the ranks of the unemployed. However, if you consistently make poor first impressions in business, it can create a stigma that can be hard to shake. Why are first impressions so important? When we first meet people, we judge them on a number of factors, including:

- Their physical appearance.
- How they are dressed.
- Their posture.
- Their apparent level of self-confidence.
- Their ability to communicate (speak articulately and listen actively).
- Their social graces.
- Their smiles.
- The nonverbal signals they send (positive, negative, harmonious).
- Their eye contact.
- What they resonate.

We then filter all of the above items through our own unique mental filter and conclude one of the following:

- I like this person.
- I don't like this person.
- I respect this person.
- I don't respect this person.
- I trust this person.
- I don't trust this person.
- I accept this person at face value.
- I sense that this person has some hidden agendas.

Things such as a genuine smile; a firm handshake; confident, open body language; good, erect posture; appropriate eye contact; attentiveness; good verbal skills; appropriate attire; good hygiene; genuine interest; and a good attitude contribute to a positive or favorable first impression.

Too much talking; not paying attention; uncomfortable demeanor; bad posture; lack of adequate eye contact; inattention; and an "uninspiring handshake" all contribute to an unfavorable impression.

In short, stand or sit up straight, smile, maintain eye contact, know of what you speak, listen, and look good. The rest will take care of itself.

Develop a Slight Edge

More than thirty years ago, while I was a distributor for a major franchise organization, I was introduced to the slight-edge concept. Being in my mid-twenties and having had little exposure at that point with "motivation and personal development," this concept was a revolutionary idea to me. Today, many of you may be familiar with both, either formally or informally. But just what is the slight edge, and how do you obtain it?

In sports, in business, in education—in all walks of life—the person or organization who wins (however they choose to define winning—not necessarily beating someone else but perhaps by beating your own previous best) isn't necessarily one hundred or even ten times better. They just tend to be a little better at the

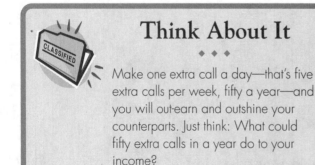

Think About It

• • •

Make one extra call a day—that's five extra calls per week, fifty a year—and you will out-earn and outshine your counterparts. Just think: What could fifty extra calls in a year do to your income?

important things. They are generally not extraordinary people or organizations—they just do the little things in an extraordinary way. Let me give you an example.

The hitter in baseball that hits over a .300 batting average will earn at least ten times as much in income as the player who only hits .250. The difference is one more hit every twenty times at bat. That's it! You don't have to be insanely productive to be a superstar. Simply exceed expectations and the competition—whoever or whatever your competition may be—on a consistent basis and BINGO—you are a super success! It doesn't take a major sacrifice. Just routinely do a little more each day and watch the balance sheet add up.

Integrity and Ethics

The sales profession today needs people with integrity, honesty, and the ability to develop trusting relationships with customers, support staff, suppliers, and management. Read the following story and decide whether integrity rules in this scenario.

Randy, a new salesperson for the ABC Company, meets with a prospect. The prospect, Barbara, asks if Randy's product or service will satisfy their basic problem, which is high product costs.

Be a Star

What little things can you do each day to outshine your competition? Try these steps to stay one step ahead:

- Make an extra telephone call.
- Obtain one more referral.
- Study your product or your job, one more hour.
- Work in an additional appointment.
- Make one more closing attempt.

Randy affirms that his product will solve their problem. After discussing all of the features and benefits, Randy quotes a price for his product.

At this point Barbara resists, saying that she does not have enough money in her budget for this service even though she needs it to reduce costs. She understands that she needs it and that his product will solve her problem. She just doesn't have the money. Randy's response is to recommend a lesser version of the product that she can afford, saying it will work just as well. (It really won't satisfy all of her concerns or needs, but he wants the sale, and justifies his action by thinking that Barbara's taking the lesser version is better than doing nothing.) She is concerned that by going to a lesser version, she will be sacrificing the ability to totally satisfy her need and solve her problem. Randy assures her it will work, that this version only lacks a few of the bells and whistles of the original recommendation, and that she will lose nothing of real importance. He closes the sale.

What do you think? Is our sales friend lacking integrity? Is it okay, from time to time, to tell just a little white lie that doesn't do major harm to the relationship? If it is okay to tell little white ones, when or under what circumstances are they acceptable? Ethics is a major issue for many people, including customers, vendors, and prospects. What are your standards? Do you stick to the truth no matter how hard it might hurt you now or the outcome later?

Truth at all costs? Is it a matter of personal perspective? Many people, sooner or later, in an attempt to protect themselves or another person from pain, disappointment, or to avoid conflict, will lie. However,

In my opinion, truth, although it might cost you a sale, is always the best policy.

when you do, you set the relationship up for failure. Misrepresentation, shading the truth, little white fibs, or outright lies can never help you in your sales career or with a client relationship. In my opinion, truth, although it might cost you the sale, is always the best policy. It was Mark Twain who said, "When you tell the truth you never have to remember what you said." Amen.

People Buy from People They Trust

Over the years, of course, much has changed in the sales environment. Nevertheless, one thing is and always will be a certainty: People buy from people they trust. Your product is an extension of you. If a customer can trust you, then the customer can trust buying your product from you.

So has anything changed in selling over the past fifty years? Those of you who have been selling for less than five years most likely will answer that question with a "no." Those of you with battle scars going back to the 1960s, 1970s, and even the 1980s may answer with a resounding "a whole lot." Some of you are just not sure or can't articulate what the changes have been. As you begin your sales career, you might want to make a mental note of the following changes and current realities of the sales profession:

- People have better, quicker, and easier access to information about your products and services and those of your competitors.
- People want you to help them make better informed decisions.
- There are three major segments of prospects: millions of baby boomers, millions of retired folks, and millions of people under the age of thirty-five who have lots and lots of money.
- More women are in positions of influence with respect to purchases.
- There are increased opportunities to sell to people from different cultures.

Think About It

• • •

You attract to yourself a reflection of your own values, beliefs, expectations, and attitudes.

- There are fewer layers of management to go through to get to your decision-maker.
- Technology is changing buyer–buying patterns and attitudes.
- People will not tolerate poor quality or poor service. Instead, they will do business with your competitor.
- Your prospects have an increasing number of options, choices, and vendors from whom to buy what they need.

Not everything has changed. Some things are tried-and-true and are here to stay:

- People buy what they want and desire.
- People want a fair value.
- People do not want to be lied to or misled.
- People do not want to pay too much to solve their problem or satisfy their wants and needs.

Life Is Perceptual

No one looks at life, its events, conditions, or circumstances in the same way. We see life not as it is, but as we are. Each of us has a mental filter through which we interpret other people's behavior, events, and circumstances. Ten people can look at the same piece of art, the same auto accident, movie, or sunset and see it differently. This gives life diversity and its relationships their challenges. Each of us has a mental filter with which we filter all of the experiences and observations in our life. For example: If I asked you to give me the opinion of this book so far, your comments would be completely your own and different from everyone else who has read the book. No one would describe its style, content, or objectives exactly the same.

One example I use in my seminar on relationships for couples is the idea of faults. Do you know someone who has faults? Be honest now. Look closely at them for a moment. Aren't another person's faults what that person thinks, feels, believes, or does differently than what you think they should feel, think, believe, or act? The assumption you are making when another person has a fault is that your way of feeling, acting, and so forth is either better than theirs or more correct.

- People buy from people they trust.
- People do not buy just because they like you—you must fill a want or need of theirs.

The world is constantly changing, and the sales profession is no different. Keeping up with and even ahead of the times is often one of the elements that makes for an extraordinary salesperson. So study and stay up to date, and you will remain ahead of your competition.

How to Be the Salesperson You Want to Be

We have talked about some of the qualities you need—integrity, professionalism, willingness to work hard, and others—to be a successful salesperson. But you also need to know of some common mistakes

There is no right or wrong, only differences in perception. This is one of the biggest issues in sales relationships that causes stress and conflict. The need to change the other person to your way of thinking arises because you think that theirs is wrong and yours is right. Acceptance is one of the biggest hurdles people face in relationships. It is also a major issue when it comes to motivating ourselves on a consistent basis. If we fail to perceive life and its events and people clearly, we will tend to fall into a number of de-motivating traps such as guilt, blame, resentment, anger, and any number of other negative emotions or feelings. These negative responses will color your use of your talent and how you treat others on a regular basis.

One of the best indicators of someone who is happy, successful, and living with their world in a harmonious way is how clearly he or she is in touch with reality—not their reality, but *actual* reality. Truth is, it is not *our* interpretation of reality, and yet so many people believe that their truth should be everyone's truth.

Think about this: Where are your perceptions about life, selling, people, events, circumstances, your past, present, or future clouded? Where do you need a clearer vision and more accurate perceptual integrity?

salespeople make, some of the myths that may cloud the reality of sales, and how to handle the unfortunate, but inevitable, moments of rejection.

Common Sales Mistakes

The marketplace is filled with poor and unprofessional salespeople. The sales profession is no different than any other when it comes to having its share of exceptional professionals as well as those people who could tarnish the reputation of the profession at large. Although many of the following traits are not perceived as unprofessional or unethical, they certainly go a long way to put salespeople—all of us—in a less than desirable light. And they are absolutely characteristics and actions that you don't want to perpetrate, at least if you want to be able to afford a hot meal. Poor salespeople:

- Talk too much.
- Give information before they get information.
- Fail to observe and integrate early prospect signals.
- Don't effectively manage rejection and failure.
- Sell when they should prospect and prospect when they should sell.
- Don't listen and take notes while the prospect is talking.
- Inject their own values, and perhaps buying prejudices, into the sales process.
- Don't effectively read buyers' signals and act accordingly.
- Sell features and price rather than value and customer benefits.
- Don't keep good records or evaluate their wins and losses.
- Fail to work as hard to keep the business as they did to get it.
- Don't ask for the business.

- Focus on making the sale rather than selling the relationship.
- Don't invest enough time and money in their self-development.
- Confuse the importance of knowing with that of caring.
- Misrepresent their products, services, or both.
- Have poor knowledge of their product, service, or both.
- Don't realize that they represent their organization and profession 24/7.
- Fail to honor their commitments.
- Are unprofessional in their behavior and demeanor.

When I was a new salesperson, one of the biggest mistakes I ever made occurred during an appointment with the president of one of my company's biggest clients. During the middle of my presentation I had to use the rest room. I excused myself right in the middle of the interview to go to the bathroom, which of course, was extremely disruptive and reflected poorly on me. So always use the rest room before you begin an appointment, or at the very least, limit your beverage intake before the appointment.

Always use the rest room before you begin an appointment, or at the very least, limit your beverage intake leading up to the appointment.

Common Sales Myths

Over the years, a great number of sales trainers, as well as sales managers, have perpetuated a number of sales myths. They may have been true at the time they were invented, created, or thought up, or at least thought to be true. It is my belief, though, that in today's global economy, where change, technology, and value are driving consumers to new levels of need satisfaction and understanding, that these myths are no longer true no matter who is preaching them. I would like to share just a few of these with you and my reasoning as to why they are myths, not truths, and what the truth really is. Decide for yourself what makes the most sense to you, what you may have heard as you began your career, or what feels right to you.

Myth: *Sales is a numbers game.*

Truth: *Sales is not a numbers game.* It is not a game at all. Selling is serious business. If you see enough people, you will make enough sales. Bull. Selling *is* a quality numbers game. If you see enough of the right people (qualified prospects), you will make lots of sales. The rationale here is that the number-one cause of failure in sales is the issue of rejection. If your strategy is to see lots of people, qualified or otherwise, sooner or later you are going to get more rejection than you can probably handle and will either quit or fail. This approach is not designed to give you permission to not make lots of calls. It is, however, designed to ensure that you spend your valuable selling time with good prospects.

Myth: *Salespeople can never give too much information.*

Truth: *Poor salespeople talk too much.* They give information *before* they get it. If this is your approach, you will tend to make one of two mistakes: giving unnecessary information, or giving wrong information. Selling is not about giving a presentation filled with features and benefits that your organization has decided are important for the prospect to know. It is about giving only that information that each prospect (and they are all different) wants or needs to make an informed and intelligent buying decision.

Think About It

◆ ◆ ◆

Your prospect's enthusiasm for your product or service is in direct proportion to your own enthusiasm.

This is the difference between an organization or product-driven focus and a customer-driven focus.

Myth: *You can fake it until you make it.*

Truth: *Successful salespeople spend their time learning, growing, reading, observing, and developing habits, attitudes, approaches, and techniques that work.* They know what works because their purpose is to be good at what they do. If your approach is to fake it while you are learning, sooner or later you will get caught, and in my experience, it is sooner rather than later and more often versus less often.

Myth: *In every sales presentation or appointment you need some small talk, or a warming up-period.*

Truth: *Each prospect deserves a unique and custom-designed sales approach based on his or her personality and style.* Some people want and need warm-up time, but others don't. The key is not to use the same approach with everyone, but to learn which approach is appropriate on each call.

> *The key is not to use the same approach with everyone, but to learn which approach is appropriate on each call.*

Myth: *I only need to hear six more no's from poor prospects, and the next one is sure to buy!*

Truth: *You can hear one hundred straight no's and still hear no from the next person, too.* You can also get seven straight yes's (closed sales) if you are calling on good prospects.

Myth: *People buy from people they like!*

Truth: *People buy from people they trust.*

Myth: *People buy because of your product's features!*

Truth: *People buy because your product or service solves a problem for them, answers a need, want, or desire, or offers an opportunity for gain.*

Myth: *Everyone buys your products and services for the same reasons!*

Truth: *People buy from you for their reasons, not yours.*

Myth: *You can sell anybody anything!*

Truth: *You can't close everyone.* If you have been selling for at least a month, you have figured this out already.

Myth: *Everyone is a prospect for you!*

Truth: *You must seek and find viable prospects.*

Myth: *The close is the most important part of the sales process!*

Truth: *Prospecting and qualifying are the most important.*

Myth: *The best salespeople make the best sales managers!*

Truth: *It requires more than good sales skills to be a good manager.*

Myth: *People always want the lowest price!*

Truth: *People do not want to spend more than they need to, but they really want the highest value (lowest cost to them over time).*

Myth: *Salespeople are born, not made!*

Truth: *Successful salespeople develop their skills and attitudes. They are not born with these.*

Myth: *Everyone buys a product or service for the same reason.*

Truth: *Not everyone has the same sense of pain, urgency, or desire.*

Psychological Debt

More than thirty years ago, when I was failing in my first sales position and struggling every step of the way, I had an important mentor in my life who gave me the most valuable insight I have ever gained in my entire sales career. Here is a very condensed version of a conversation that took place in the early 1960s.

"Larry, I don't understand it. Everyone I give a presentation to tells me how good I am, how knowledgeable I am, and how successful he or she believes I will be in selling. But they still don't buy."

"Tim, you are experiencing what I call psychological debt."

"What's that?"

"During a presentation, you do a lot for a prospect. You give them your time, energy, the benefits of your insight, wisdom, and experience. You are nice to them, and you educate them. In other words, you do a great deal for them in the span of an hour or so."

"What's your point, Larry?"

Don't Shoot Yourself in the Foot

Many salespeople could be so much more successful than they are. All they need is a willingness to stop behaviors that hurt their success and replace them with actions and attitudes that will ensure success. What are some of the factors that limit salespeople's success? They include:

- Believing that success in selling will be easy and fast.
- The inability to keep motivated regardless of the circumstances.
- Living in the past or the future.
- A lack of consistent effort.
- Letting yourself off the hook when you fail to reach your goals.

"A little impatient aren't we? You see, Tim, you have done a lot for them, and they feel they owe you, psychologically, that is. And they don't want you leaving, owing you, and they don't want to buy for whatever reason, so they give you a compliment. Once you accept the compliment, the debt is paid, and you can leave without an order, but supposedly feeling good about yourself because of the compliment. Problem is, sooner or later, with lots of compliments and no sales, you will starve. You'll feel good, but you will be broke."

"So what do I do?"

"It's simple. When you get an order and a compliment, say thank you. When you get a compliment instead of an order, refuse the compliment. Then the debt still exists. Here's how: 'Bob, if I were that good at what I do, we would be doing business together today, and since we are not, I'm afraid I don't deserve that compliment.'"

"Tim, younger and new salespeople tend to have a problem with this issue. Since they are new, they have a need for validation, acceptance, and approval. When they get it, it strokes their ego, their need for acceptance and makes them feel okay. Problem is, if they don't deal with it successfully, they will fail. You can't pay your mortgage with compliments."

I haven't seen Larry in more than thirty-five years, but his advice has helped me avoid losing hundreds of sales during my career. Thanks, Larry—wherever you are.

- A lack of clear focus, direction, and goals.
- Inadequate planning time.
- Not investing enough time and cash in yourself, your skills, and your attitude development.
- Low goals.
- A failure to manage rejection and failure with a positive attitude.
- Turning the responsibility for your success over to someone else: your company, the economy, your boss, or anyone.
- An out-of-control ego.

During my first year in sales, when I was selling advertising, I recall not following up on a client to see if he was satisfied with our services. Three months into his contract, he canceled the order. I called and asked him why he was canceling. He said, "The program isn't working." I said, "Why didn't you call me to tell me?" He said, "Why didn't you call me sooner to find out whether it was working?"

Think About It

• • •

Keep your focus on what you want, can do, or have, not what you don't want, don't have, or can't do.

Another valuable lesson learned, folks.

Of course, the most important thing is learning what to do to prevent these self-sabotaging attitudes or behaviors:

- Get up an hour earlier every day and spend the time planning your day, year, career, or life.
- Start investing 10 percent of your income and time in self-development.
- Start a personal goal-setting journal and live it—every day.

- Develop a greater degree of patience, faith, and trust in yourself and the world.
- Give yourself away a little every day: your time, ideas, energy, or other assets.
- Count your blessings and live with gratitude for what you have.
- Take full responsibility for your life, yourself, your career, your future, your past. Take full responsibility for everything in your life.
- Kill your ego.
- Accept the reality that not everyone you meet, try to sell to, or whatever, is going to like you. It's just not that kind of world.
- Relax and enjoy the ride.
- Embrace change and let go of attachments to the past.
- Start a good stuff jar.
- Work as if you will live forever, and live as if you will die today.

Managing Rejection

What is the number-one cause of failure in sales? It's the inability to overcome the fear of rejection. Why do people let this fear negatively influence their behavior? Here are a few thoughts to consider that will I hope will prepare you for the inevitable rejections and prevent them from becoming commonplace:

- Not everyone you try to sell to will want to buy from you.
- Expecting everyone you meet to like or accept you is to live in fantasyland.

- If you don't ask for anything, something—it is unlikely you will ever get it.
- The fear of rejection prevents you from asking probing questions, asking for an appointment, or asking for the order.
- The fear of rejection is one of the major causes of failure in all areas of life, not only sales.
- The fear of rejection is an attitude issue and can only be overcome by strengthening other attitudes—such as confidence, self-belief, patience, trust, and your self-image.
- The fear of rejection is not a skill issue and can't be overcome with the latest self-help technique or fad that forces you to behave in ways that are not comfortable for you.
- The fear of rejection is a symptom of a need for acceptance, approval, or validation.
- The fear of rejection sends a loud nonverbal message to the other person that you lack confidence or belief in: yourself, your product or service, your ability to help them or solve their problems—or all of these things.

Of course, rejection will happen. The key is how you react to it.

Of course, rejection will happen. The key is how you react to it. Do you think about what you could have done better, learn any lessons, and forge ahead? Or, does the fear of rejection ever prevent you from:

- Picking up the phone and making that next call.
- Asking for the business.
- Asking difficult, probing questions.
- Asking for referrals.
- Asking for a bigger order.
- Asking for a letter of testimony.
- Asking for anything you want.

- Asking for more responsibility in your position or for a raise.
- Following up on a customer who has had a problem.
- Asking for an appointment with an important person.
- Asking for a cash deposit.
- Asking for a long-term contract.

If you answer yes to any of these, you need to address it immediately. You cannot succeed in the long term if common failures interfere with your ability to do your job and sell.

Failure Is Inevitable Sooner or Later

Failure is not negative, and it isn't positive either. Failure is an event. Some people fail and quit, while others fail and get better, wiser, and stronger because of failure. There is an interesting difference between people who fail and then succeed, and those who fail and then pack it in: which they decide is based entirely on their attitudes.

I have never met anyone in my career who was successful who hadn't also experienced numerous failures. To succeed, you must stretch yourself and reach beyond your previous limits, boundaries, and skills. If you do this, sooner or later you will fail. Sometimes you will even crash and burn. I've been there several times, my friend, but I am still here—still selling, still writing, and still failing. I love to fail. When I am not experiencing temporary failure, it is a clear message that I may be stuck in my comfort zone.

Learn to use failure, adversity, problems, and risk as tools for self-improvement rather than reasons to whine and complain.

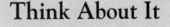

Think About It

♦ ♦ ♦

Learn to fail often so you can succeed sooner. If you are not failing, you have to ask yourself: Am I stretching, reaching, and going beyond my limits, or am I stuck in that which is comfortable?

Accept the fact that people who succeed must often first fail. Their failures give them the confidence, character, humility, and courage they will need to succeed. Success is not easy.

Frank Betcher, one of the great sales speakers of the last century put it this way, "The price of failure is always higher than the price of success. It always costs more to fail than to succeed. So, use your failures as learning opportunities."

Failures! Bring 'em on. Get ready to learn, grow, and stretch. Get out of your comfort zone and watch yourself accomplish great things.

Personal Traits for Success

As a new salesperson in your organization, you will have to meet a number of expectations for your attitudes, behaviors, and habits. You now represent your organization in the marketplace. Whether you are working, travelling, or off duty, your behavior will be closely observed by your prospects, customers, fellow employees, support staff, and suppliers. It is critical that your behavior is always professional and above reproach. You never know who is watching.

Relationship Skills and Attitudes

During your first year, you will form many new relationships. I recall in my second sales position, selling insurance, and one of my fellow salespeople—he also happened to be our number-one salesperson— told me I would never make it in the business. At the time, I didn't

Great Expectations

You will be expected to:

- Learn quickly.
- Adapt to the personality of your organization.
- Work hard.
- Work smart.
- Communicate questions, concerns, and needs.
- Accept corporate policies and operate within their guidelines.
- Know the marketplace.
- Learn about your competitors, their products and services, and their strengths and weaknesses.
- Sell.
- Dress appropriately.
- Behave professionally.

A lot to expect, yes, but you are representing their entire previous investment in public relations, reputation, and success up to this point. You now have a role as an ambassador for them and it is vital that you take this role seriously.

know why he felt the need to share his pessimistic view about my future with me. In hindsight, it was pure insecurity and jealousy. I was on track to replace his number-one status in the office and in the company, and he knew it.

Chances are, you won't run into anyone who is so blatantly negative to your face. But trust me: Sooner or later you will discover advocates as well as saboteurs. All you can do is be yourself, be friendly, and know that sooner or later, results talk. It's called leverage. When you are new and just beginning to find your way down the path of success, you will stumble in some of your relationships. Just learn from your mistakes. Before you know it, you, too, will be one of the superstars.

Continue Your Personal Development

Continued self-development is an attitude, not an event. Don't think of taking a course, reading a book, listening to a tape, or attending a sales seminar as a one-time activity. Self-improvement is a lifestyle. Lifelong learning is a philosophy that will pay you handsome dividends over time.

One approach I implemented early in my sales career was to invest 10 percent of my time and 10 percent of my income—on a weekly, monthly, and yearly basis—in my personal growth. Over time this investment will repay you thousands of times over.

Think of yourself as an independent contractor. You are selling your time, skills, attitudes, and effort to your current employer. Your value to them is represented by your income. If you want to improve your income, you must improve your value. You do that by investing in yourself. I am not talking here about attending only mandatory "company-sponsored" learning programs. I am asking you: What are you doing on your own with your own available resources?

If you want to improve your income, you must improve your value.

If your organization did not continuously improve its products or services, it would fail in the marketplace. If you do not invest in yourself, you may reach a point in your career where you are no longer able to increase your income, simply because your value has not increased. Develop the habit—in your first year—of investing regularly in yourself, and specifically, in your skills and attitudes.

The Importance of Motivation and Goal Setting

Motivation is a very personal issue. Research has concluded that everyone has the potential for great motivation, but not everyone is willing to pay the motivational price to achieve their dreams, desires, or hopes. Many people fail to really ask themselves one critical question: What motivates me?

What Motivates You?

Some of the more traditional motivators are:

- Money.
- Security.
- Fame.
- Power.
- Prestige.
- Ego gratification.
- Winning.
- Being the best.
- Doing your best.
- Your family.
- Your future.
- Your past.
- Not losing.
- Personal satisfaction.
- Approval of others.
- To prove a point.
- To get even.
- To feel worthwhile.
- To impress others.

Do any of these drive you? Keep you going when you are on the verge of quitting, giving up, or throwing in the towel?

For years, thousands of managers, hundreds of speakers and trainers, and dozens of authors have been preaching the benefits and value of self-motivation and goals as a way to achieve success, wealth, and happiness. And for good reason. Find what motivates you and pushes you to strive for the top, and keep that in mind when the going gets tough or you simply need or want to reach a higher level. A motivator is one of your tools for success.

But just as there are motivators, there are de-motivators. A de-motivator is anything—a person, circumstance, situation—that acts upon you, causing your interpretation and subsequent behavior to be negative, passive, or self-destructive.

Fortunately, there are tangible ways to address self-motivation. Six basic steps will allow you to reach your peak performance behavior and results when it comes to self-motivation:

1. Know what you want.
2. Know why you want it.
3. Know how you will get it.

4. Know what may stand in your way to achieve it (external obstacles: circumstances, people, events; internal obstacles: attitudes, emotions, fears, and doubts).

5. Be aware of the outside-in and inside-out de-motivators and develop a plan to deal with them, prevent them, or manage them.

6. Do something. Begin. Start.

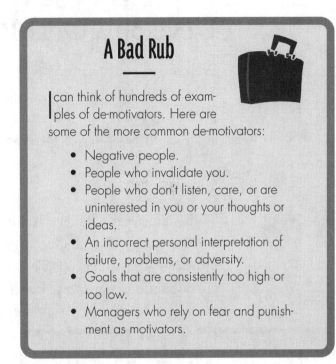

A Bad Rub

I can think of hundreds of examples of de-motivators. Here are some of the more common de-motivators:

- Negative people.
- People who invalidate you.
- People who don't listen, care, or are uninterested in you or your thoughts or ideas.
- An incorrect personal interpretation of failure, problems, or adversity.
- Goals that are consistently too high or too low.
- Managers who rely on fear and punishment as motivators.

De-motivators come in all shapes and sizes. They can be your personal demons that no one but you is ever aware of, or they can be a corporate policy or family rule that contributes to an "I don't care anymore" attitude. Apathy is one of the most destructive human emotions when it comes to performance, productivity, happiness, success, motivation, and overall behavior.

Audit Your De-Motivators

Conduct an internal as well as external self-audit of your de-motivators. Identify them, question their purpose and value in your life, decide if it is time to rid yourself of their power over you or learn to live with the consequences of keeping them in your life. One of the best ways to improve self-motivation and personal performance is to eliminate the de-motivators from your life, whatever form they take.

Develop a Goal Philosophy

Even a goal to do nothing is a goal. Everyone has goals. They just define them and move toward or away from them with a variety of perspectives or rationales. There are two primary reasons for setting goals: First, they give you focus; second, they give you direction.

Focus

Without focus, it is difficult to hit a bulls-eye, take a good picture, or avoid getting killed on a busy highway. Focus is an essential characteristic of successful people. It keeps your eye on the ball. Yes, there are distractions, unexpected circumstances, and unknowns that will impact your ability to keep your focus, but focus you must.

Think About It

• • •

Personal organization is defined differently by each of us. The key is, can you be productive with your current organizational style?

Direction

The ultimate achievement of a goal is less important than the ability to continue working toward it. Many people achieve their goals and are disappointed once they reach them. A goal once achieved is a milestone, yes, but you can't just sit back and rest on your previous success.

When winners don't reach a goal, they re-examine what needs to change and then changes the time frame to achieve it. When losers don't reach goals, they re-examine and then change the goal.

Don't worry about the destination. Keep your eye on the ball in the present with what you can do now, not tomorrow. Do something every day to move a little closer to your objective. Remember that while you can't have everything in your life that you want, you can have anything. Keep the understanding of this principle clear in your mind.

To set goals and not put accountability into the process is like whistling in the wind. You are living in fantasyland if you think you will achieve your goals if you have not made progress toward them and you do not have some checkpoints along the way.

At every checkpoint, you should consider:

1. Are you satisfied with your progress toward your goals?
2. If not, which ones are you behind on? Why?
3. Are you ahead of schedule on any of your goals? Which ones? Why?
4. Is it time to let go of any of your goals?
5. Is it time to add some new goals to this year's list?
6. Who or what is affecting your negative goal progress?
7. Who or what is impacting your positive goal progress?
8. If you could go back to last year and begin this goal-setting process all over again, would you have done anything differently?
9. What are you going to change in the next three months to ensure you are on target for your important goals?

How to Set and Reach Your Goals

Not only must you create goals, you must decide ahead of time the best way to reach them. Of course, the best way to reach a goal may change over time, which is why progress evaluations are so important. First things first, though. As you go through the process of setting ambitious yet reasonable goals, you must consider the following:

*   Set time deadlines for your goals.

- Know the difference between tangible and intangible goals.
- Reward yourself when you reach a goal.
- Update them at least once a year.
- Share mutual goals with other people who can help you, influence you, or will be impacted by them.
- Set both short- (hourly to six months) and long-term goals (six months to lifetime).
- Record your accomplished goals in a journal.
- Be willing to abandon a goal when you have lost interest.
- Accept the fact that patience and faith are virtues.
- Know your reasons for wanting to reach a goal.
- Relax and enjoy the process.
- Life is not about the result, but the process of becoming.
- Accept the fact that you can't do it all, have it all, learn it all, see it all, become it all, or share it all in one lifetime.
- Goal setting is not a short-term fix, but a lifetime philosophy.
- Life can change in a heartbeat.
- Goals change as your interests, age, and circumstances change.
- Don't edit the goal-setting process as you proceed thorough the steps. (I don't have the time now. I can't afford it now, etc.) Don't worry about being realistic in the beginning. The purpose of the process is to add realism as you go.
- Goals should be achievable, but also require some stretch.
- Get in the habit of working on paper with your goal setting.
- Recognize that achieving goals takes effort, commitment, time, and skills.

The Importance of Balancing Your Career and Personal Life

Balance in life means many things to each of us. There are entire books written on the subject. Here are a few of the critical factors of a balanced life:

- Move consistently and purposely toward meaningful goals in all seven areas of your life (page 55).

- Live in the present—one moment at a time. The present is where your plans are made, memories are created, and relationships built.

- Live life from the inside-out, not the outside-in; take full personal responsibility for the quality of your existence.

- Let go of your old emotional baggage. It keeps you stuck in the past and prevents you from experiencing true joy in living.

- Accept the fact that life just is! It is not perfect. Everyone has their share of pain, problems, disappointments, mistakes and struggles.

- Daily, count your blessings.

Common Contributors to a Lack of Goal Success

- Lack of commitment to the process.
- Impatience.
- Lack of follow through.
- Lack of self-honesty.
- Consistently setting goals too high.
- Not anticipating roadblocks.
- Not allowing for enough time to reach your goal.
- Setting only long-term goals.
- Setting only tangible goals.
- A lack of support, resources from people who can help you.
- Working toward a goal you don't believe in or really want.
- Not believing you will ever reach your goal.
- Quitting too soon.
- Not starting to work toward your goal.

- Live without regrets. Regret is a debt you can never pay. It will haunt you until your final day.
- Make thoughtful choices. Choices become our ultimate destiny. Wise choices create a life worth living.
- Live a simple and humble life. Keep your ego out of your actions, relationships, decisions, and plans—you will find inner peace.
- People, not things, are what really matter. In the end, it is not what you have accumulated that gives your life meaning, but rather your relationships with people.

Keep Good Records

To chart a more effective course for the future, you need to know where you have been. You need to know precisely where you must modify behavior, improve skills, or change approaches. Professional salespeople ask themselves regularly, "What is working, what isn't working, and what used to work that I have stopped doing?" They keep immaculate records on activity, results, errors, mistakes, successes, and anything else they need to improve. Whether they use a journal, a spreadsheet, or some type of call report doesn't matter. What matters is that they can bring their personal history into their present, therefore changing their future.

Professional salespeople ask themselves regularly, "What is working, what isn't working, and what used to work that I have stopped doing?"

Many sales managers and sales organizations require call reports of your activity and results. See these as an opportunity to improve, not as a waste of your time. Take them seriously. In addition to these reports, whether daily, weekly, or monthly, I also suggest you keep additional records of your: successes, problems, challenges, needs, activities, questions, concerns—whatever will help you keep track of your history, progress, failures, and successes.

Causes of Sales Slumps

Sooner or later, every salesperson experiences a down period of sales results. These periods, where your continued activity seems to yield less than satisfactory results, are normal and to be expected. None of us can keep up a pace of 200 miles per hour day after day, month after month, year after year. The key is to keep your attitude positive, your focus on what is working, and your activity levels high regardless of the results.

There are a variety of sales slumps. Let's just discuss four: the attitude slump, prospecting slump, presentation slump, and the closing slump.

The Attitude Slump

An attitude slump is where you find it difficult to maintain your confidence, poise, commitment, dedication, persistence, and motivation. This can be due to a number of causes, including that you have lost belief in your organization's products or services; you are not reaching your goals or objectives according to your schedule; you are under a great deal of stress due to deadlines, expectations, or loss of control of the sales process; you have other issues in your life that are impacting your attitudes.

The Prospecting Slump

A prospecting slump is where you lack adequate qualified leads and are spending a great deal of time calling on poor prospects. As a result, your close ratio is a disaster. This could also be caused by your poor prospecting strategies; that is, you are still (after several months selling your products or services) spending a lot of time cold calling.

The Presentation Slump

You can't pull out of any of these slumps just focusing on the one area that you feel might be your problem. You have to work on all of them.

A presentation slump can be caused by your lack of up-to-date product knowledge, poor presentation skills, or poor communication skills, such as listening, speaking, or writing. This can also be caused by your lack of knowledge of the prospect's needs, use, or applications of your products or services. You therefore give an organization-driven rather than a customer-driven sales pitch.

Closing Slump

A closing slump can be caused by your lack of control of the sales process, poor prospecting, poor sales presentations, or many of the items in the attitude area that we have already discussed.

Breaking the Cycle

As you can see, there are a number of areas where you can experience a down cycle in your sales approach. The thing to consider is that all of them are related. In other words, if you are experiencing an attitude slump, it will have an impact on your prospecting, presentation, and closing. If you are in a closing slump, it will impact on your attitudes as well as other areas of the sales process.

You can't pull out of any of these slumps simply by focusing on the one area that you feel might be your problem. You have to work on all of them. The way out of a slump is to go back to what works, or has worked for you in the past. It is also an excellent time for reflection and self-evaluation of your progress, success, weaknesses, and strengths.

Becoming an Effective Salesperson

From day one, there are numerous things that you can and should do to start developing your skills and attitudes for success. From learning as much as you can about your product or service, to streamlining your responsibilities, to managing your time wisely, the sooner you have a plan and organize in your mind the most efficient and thorough methods for doing your job, the better off you will be.

Think About It

◆ ◆ ◆

Some prospects are worth more time, energy, and resources than others. The key is to know which are worthy and why.

The Importance of Product and Industry Knowledge

People need to know how much you care, but they also want and need to know that you have the competence to guide, direct, recommend, or select the best option or choice for them regarding your product or service. Product knowledge is a vital sales requirement if you are to compete successfully.

There are a variety of things you need to know from a product knowledge standpoint. You need to know:

- What your product or service does.
- What your product or service *can't* do and what it *isn't*.

- How your product or service is unique.
- How it is different from your competitors'.

This is just a start. The key is to know what you need to know and what your prospects need you to know to address their needs, questions, challenges, or problems. Winging it about product knowledge is no longer an acceptable strategy.

This is especially true when you are dealing with a complex product or service and have knowledgeable and sophisticated buyers. Don't fake product knowledge. Learn what you need to know as quickly as you can. Product knowledge does not make up for poor people skills, selling skills, or poor attitudes, but if you have all four, you can achieve greatness in sales.

Key Success Factors in Your First Year

You will have a lot to learn during the next several months. Depending on the type of sales position you're in, you will determine the key factors for your success. You will need to consider whether or not:

- It is purely an inside sales position.
- You have leads provided.
- You are taking over an existing territory.
- You will be selling a low-price service or product or a high-price one.
- You will have inside sales support.
- You will be selling an intangible service or a tangible product.
- There will be weekend or evening appointments.

How you spend your time, what obstacles you encounter, what you will have to learn, and what new habits or attitudes you need to develop will all depend on your particular unique circumstances. In this book, you will find keys to all of your challenges regardless of which ones you face.

Learn to Compartmentalize

One of the ongoing challenges for many salespeople is the ability to "compartmentalize" areas of their lives. Let me explain.

As a writer, it is important for me to be able to set aside all life challenges, issues, and problems once I sit at my computer to create and write. This setting-aside is often easier said than done, whether we're talking about a salesperson or a writer. For example, suppose your spouse just announced, after twenty-five years of marriage, he or she is leaving. Your car has just been repossessed, and your teenager is in trouble. Not a pretty picture. Fortunately, not many have this much hit us simultaneously. However, we all have our battles, big and small, that we must face on an ongoing basis. The ability to keep these issues separate while you are trying to sell is vital.

Salespeople who cannot separate their personal life challenges from their career responsibilities generally resonate out in some non-verbal or emotional way that they have problems. We all have problems. We all will always have problems. If you don't, get some quickly. Problems build character. I can just hear some-one reading this screaming—I have had enough charac-ter building. Maybe yes, maybe no. But consider this—if you still have problems anywhere in your life, you may not have built as much character as you need to fulfill your mission or destiny on this planet. When you cannot separate these personal issues from your career roles you will tend to:

Problems build character.

- Reduce your positive state of mind, which will impact your success.
- Increase your stress, which will impact your health and ability to be creative.
- Send mixed communication messages to your prospect or cus-tomer.
- Lose your competitive edge.

Following are a few steps to consider to separate the areas of your life so that one area will not have more control over another area than you chose give it:

- Focus on something positive rather than negative in the area of your life that concerns you.
- Spend time before each call or appointment in relaxation and or a short meditation period.
- Focus on your long-term life goals and your progress when life throws you a curve.
- Develop little routines or positive anchors to use when you are troubled.
- Carry some personal physical reminder with you of what is positive in your life or that area that is causing you grief or worry.
- Call someone who will give you emotional support, feedback, or just warm fuzzies to help you re-focus on what is positive.

Start Networking Your First Day

There has been a myth circulating for years about networking. It is not what you know, but who you know that will determine your success. Not so. It isn't who you know, but who knows you. I am not splitting hairs here, trust me. I know a lot of people who don't have a clue who I am. So it really comes down to how you define the word "knows."

The key to effective networking is to start. Make it a routine part of your selling and non-selling time. Join organizations where you can meet potential prospects as well as people who can refer you to potential prospects. Develop a 24/7 prospecting awareness. If you don't already have one, get a contact manager software package and input everyone you meet. Then, start a mail campaign: notes, letters, calls, and the like to those special people who you feel might one day be able to help you. More on networking in chapter 3.

Effectively Manage Your Time and Territory

My research shows that typical salespeople spend 10 to 20 percent of their time selling and 70 to 80 percent doing everything else. Isn't it amazing that you can earn an income in sales spending less than 20 percent of your time selling? Imagine what you could do to your results and income if you could increase that number by only 10 percent?

Think About It
◆ ◆ ◆

Start an advocate list of the top twenty-five people who you want to cultivate as your key support group. These people can give you ideas, feedback, help, and contacts. Select these people very carefully.

Mastering Time and Territory Management

Obviously, a productive use of time is essential. Part of using your time wisely is managing your territory efficiently.

Time management and effective time use are the result of many skills, attitudes, prejudices, habits, and personal philosophies. No one can manage time. If a person has a time-management issue or problem, it is most likely due to a weakness or lack of ability in some other area of their life, such as managing resources, people, decisions, problems, emotions, failure, activities, or success.

The Balancing Act

Each of us has numerous demands on our time, energy, and resources. One of the keys to sales success is the ability to balance multiple:

- Demands.
- Expectations of customers.
- Requirements of our position.
- Personal needs and desires.
- Tasks.
- Routine activities.
- Family roles.
- Expectations of supervisors.
- Personal growth possibilities.

It is no wonder that many salespeople burn out early in their careers due to the inability to successfully handle all of these issues, challenges, and requirements. If success is one of your agendas you will ultimately have to:

- Eliminate something from your plate.
- Better manage all of these issues and roles.
- Get better organized.
- Or live with the continued stress of poor organization.

I am sure you know the feeling of being overwhelmed—the need to satisfy everyone and everything in your life. This combines with the desire to create a sense of peace in your life knowing that—while working on other people's issues, expectations, and demands—you have not abandoned your own requirements for achievement and success. You also know how you have felt when you end a day, week, or month with a great deal of unfinished business. Everyone who hopes to do more, have more, become more, learn more, and contribute more will, sooner or later, have to confront their own needs and style of what personal organization means to them. No one can tell you how to organize your life and career. What learning can do is help you identify where growth, change, or a new philosophy is needed so you can regain some sense of harmony while climbing the ladder of personal success, whatever that means to you.

Hints for Managing Your Time

To improve time use, a person must identify these impeding tendencies, attitudes, or weaknesses and then develop skills and abilities to address and overcome them. You can't improve time use—it is a nebulous concept. I challenge anyone to manage the next minute or hour. It can't be done. However, there are a couple of must-knows about yourself that can help you maximize your time and results.

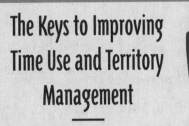

The Keys to Improving Time Use and Territory Management

- Know yourself.
- Know your tendencies.
- Know your strengths.
- Know your weaknesses.
- Know your goals.
- Identify your common time-wasters.
- Have a prospecting strategy.
- Establish regular planning times.

Know Your Prime Time

What is Prime Time? It is that time of the day, week, or month when you are at your best. Are you a morning person? Late-night person? Other? Does your energy fade during a certain time of the day or week?

Know Your Prime Time Plus

That is, the combination of time when you are at your best and your customers and prospects can see you. For example: If you are a morning person and a client or prospect wants a conference call in the morning, this is your Prime Time Plus. However, if you are an

Schedule critical sales activities during Prime Time Plus and non-sales activities during your non-Prime Time Plus.

afternoon person—your energy, creativity, and imagination peak in the mid-afternoon—and you are not at your best in the early morning, it is best to schedule your meetings in the afternoon, during your Prime Time or Prime Time Plus. The key is to schedule critical sales activities during Prime Time Plus and non-sales activities during your non-Prime Time Plus.

Time Block Approach

This strategy helps you blend the goals and objectives in your life with the available time at your disposal. It ensures that you don't neglect any area of your life while moving toward your goals and life purpose.

The Value of Lists

Working from lists is one sure way to ensure that you:

- Don't forget to do something important.
- Work on the important stuff first.
- Feel good about your day.
- End the day, week, and month without neglecting an important task, activity, or role.
- Enjoy the time you have.
- Get more satisfaction from your life's responsibilities.
- Get more done.
- Sell more.

You start with a month or week. You list your top five or ten goals in the important segments of your life in all or some of the following areas:

- Family.
- Career.
- Finances.
- Socializing.
- Education.
- Physical needs.
- Spiritual needs.

Start with a clean month or week. Nothing included. Now take your number-one priority, whether it be time with a spouse, exercise, reading, sales appointments, or something else. Block out the time for this area in the week or month. Now go to your second priority.

Work from lists of things *to do*. Here's how:

1. Make a list.
2. Prioritize the items on the list according to your goals, needs, desires, activities, and demands.
3. Start with the important ones (must do's) first.
4. Finish these before you move to the less important ones (should do's)
5. Finish these before you move to the unimportant ones (will do if I get time)

Work from lists, and you will get more done in less time. As a result, you'll have more time for planning, contemplation, reflection, relaxation, fun, and thought. All valuable activities that, while often overlooked, can give you an additional edge and forethought.

Develop the habit of spending a certain amount of time each day, week, month, and year in solitude or as mini breaks for recharging your battery. It doesn't matter if it is a walk in the park, a slow, relaxing meal, meditation time, or just sitting down and doing nothing.

Continue to fill in blocks of time in your schedule according to your top goals, priorities, or interests. As the week and month fill, you now become acutely aware of how precious your time is and how you want and need to spend it.

Begin with the first month now, and all you have to do is translate this information to your weekly or daily list of things to do. Another way to approach it is to take a year. Using the same philosophy, block out weeks, months, or days for critical tasks, responsibilities, and activities. Become more detailed as you move from the year to a month, week, or day.

This process ensures that you don't neglect any important area of your life as you live it. Your career, personal life, financial concerns, social interests, family, and personal needs get the attention they deserve.

The Joys of Journaling

Start a journal. There are a number of outstanding reasons to keep a journal. Here are a few of them. A journal can:

- Increase your effectiveness.
- Help you learn from your failures.
- Improve your relationships.
- Help you achieve your goals.
- Keep you headed in the right direction.
- Help you learn from others.
- Save you time.
- Reduce your stress.

Keeping a record of your insights, thoughts, ideas, successes, mistakes, errors, achievements, and failures and their causes will do more for your career than any other single activity.

Realities

Paperwork is not going away, not in this lifetime anyway. It doesn't matter how technically oriented your organization becomes, there will always be paper reports: information to share, something to write, forms to complete, reports to evaluate or analyze, and some piece of paper that finds its way to your desk or mailbox. The key is to determine honestly and effectively whether you want or need to spend time on this stuff, or whether you can discard it without negative consequences. Let's take a brief look at a few of the paperwork demands on your time:

- Expense reports.
- Call reports.
- Territory reports.
- Customer reports.
- Customer history reports.
- Forecasting reports.
- Goal or quota reports.
- Competitor evaluations.

Here are a few ideas to consider while managing paper:

- It is a myth to believe that you can handle each piece of paper once.
- Technology will never replace someone's need or desire to have a hard copy of something.
- Depending on who wants the information—a customer, your boss, a fellow employee, or another department—will determine your attention span and response time.
- Most people are not good communicators on paper. They either go on and on with endless drivel, or they give us far too little information to help us make a decision.
- You need a priority system for handling your administrative tasks.
- File any notes you take during telephone conversations or appointments.
- Establish a reading file.
- Use expandable file pockets instead of hanging folders.
- Keep your briefcase organized.
- Have an effective follow-up system.

- Have an effective suspense action system.
- Do difficult tasks first thing in the day.
- Use a pencil for scheduling appointments.
- Confirm all appointments.
- Send yourself e-mails as reminders.

Territory Management

Territory management is the ability to maximize your results, reach your goals, and effectively build your business in your territory while satisfying the demands and expectations of your management team and customers. There are several keys to this.

Let's take a brief look at a few of the issues that will require your attention as you attempt to better organize your time, territory, career, and life.

Streamlining Paperwork

Here are some tips that will make your life significantly easier and free up your time for the good stuff:

- Allocate a specific amount of non-selling time to administrative requirements.
- Don't let paperwork and reports get in the way of you Prime-Time selling activities.
- Make a daily or weekly appointment with yourself for reports and paperwork.
- Categorize your administrative tasks into must do immediately, as soon as possible, to do after completing the previous.
- Form the habit of keeping daily records so at the end of the week it isn't as big a chore to complete a report or an administrative task or function.
- Organize your routine tasks such as reports and your various roles in such a way that they can be completed easily.
- Delegate what you can to a subordinate, staff person, or another department.
- Have your mail screened by a support person.

Improving Your Territory Management

One of the key characteristics in effective territory management is to do a better job of qualifying prospects prior to giving them your time, energy, or corporate resources.

Let's look at a few ways to better manage your resource of time and territory management:

1. Ask more effective questions earlier in the sales process.
2. Pay attention to their answers to determine whether it is a good time to try and sell to this prospect.
3. Develop a customer profile to use as a template for your prospecting.
4. Audit your sales call activity by dividing the number of calls you make in a week by the number of miles you drive in that week. This number will give you your call-route effectiveness.

- Create files for your paperwork: routine, urgent, archive, action today, action this week, action this month, suspense, action this year, pending, to review, to read, when I get time, from my boss, customer requests. Get creative here— the more you have, the easier it is to keep track of everything.
- Subscribe to a book review program.
- Spend a half-day each week or month in the library catching up on industry information/trends.
- Write responses on memos/faxes/e-mails rather than creating a new document.
- Keep things brief, short, and to the point. Avoid editorializing.
- Keep your memos, reports, and correspondence accurate, not perfect.
- Develop a standard format or template for all of your routine reports.
- Have a self-rating system for how well you think you are doing managing your paperwork.
- Develop the habit of asking yourself: Do I need to do this? Do I need to do it now?
- Can someone else do this?

Efficient Versus Effective

It is important to know the difference between two words: "effective" and "efficient."

Efficient means to do things well or right.

Effective means to do the right things well or right.

Note the difference? It is one thing to end your day tired due to the business of completing your list of activities. It is another thing to end your day having completed the important things—those things that needed to get done, and not just those things you wanted to do because they were easy, fun, or new.

5. Spend more prospecting time getting referrals.
6. Develop strategic alliances to help you improve your prospecting activity.
7. Plan your call activities early in the week, month, or day.
8. Don't give poor prospects more time than they deserve.
9. Develop a daily checklist of what you will need to do to be effective.
10. Try to get more of your prospects to visit your location, plant, or office.
11. Don't spend time giving presentations to people who aren't the ones who make the decisions.

Territory management, like time management, is a function of many attitudes, habits, values, skills, and beliefs. It is also a function of the:

- Geographic size of the territory.
- Number of clients and prospects in the territory.
- Method of travel through the territory; that is, air, car, or whatever.
- Non-sales responsibilities within the territory.
- Degree of administrative sales support.

To effectively manage a sales territory, it is critical that a salesperson has a prospecting strategy—a rationale for how much time, energy, and resources to give to each type of prospect or customer.

Many salespeople travel hundreds of unnecessary miles each week or month and still do not effectively "cover" their territory. Without this prospecting strategy, it is impossible to get better use of one's time and have effective territory coverage.

We have evaluated your attitudes, expectations, and reasons for beginning your sales career. We have looked at your motivation, goals, and personal organization. Now the real work begins. It is time to put much of what you have learned in chapter 1 and chapter 2 into practice. So let's get to it. Don't stop now: You're on a roll.

Attitudes and Time and Territory Management

What are some common time and territory management attitudes? How about:

- There is always tomorrow.
- There are too many demands made on my time.
- There is too much paperwork.
- My geographic territory is too large.
- I have too many prospects, customers, or both.

Politics of Sales

Every profession, every position in any organization, will have a certain amount of politics that you will have to learn to manage if you are going to make your first year successful without an unnecessary amount of negative stress. Many people dislike playing political games; however, learning to play these games effectively is an important skill that you must master during your first year in this profession.

What to Expect

During my sales career, I encountered a wide variety of political challenges that often came very close to permanently derailing me professionally. But I made it because I learned the skills and developed the attitudes that guaranteed my survival. Each of us must confront our own personal issues. Each of us will face unique circumstances as we learn the ropes in this profession.

Each organization and sales culture is unique. Some management philosophies embrace and honor the salespeople who represent their products and services in the marketplace. Others, unfortunately, regard salespeople as a necessary evil. In these organizations, management is always playing with sales territories, compensation plans, rules, procedures, policies, and strategies, often with the objective of keeping their salespeople's incomes within certain acceptable parameters. I have always held that one of the opportunities of this profession is the ability to determine your own income and destiny. Any organization that limits your financial growth and income has an agenda to keep you within historical income guidelines. If you find yourself in such a company, I am not suggesting that you become a crusader your first year and attempt to change your organization's philosophy. But you need to become aware of this manipulative political tactic.

Specific Politics and Issues

There are other political issues you will have to learn to handle. As mentioned previously, what you specifically encounter will depend a lot on the organization you work for. Nevertheless, there are certain issues that are quite common, and no doubt you will come across several of the following situations.

Department Rivalries. One of the common rivalries is the conflict between the finance and sales departments. The finance department is driven by lower sales costs and higher margins. Often, in sales, you will have to sacrifice profit margins to close a deal. Often you will have to "spend money to make money." Unfortunately, this rubs the controller, accountants, and other finance personnel the wrong way, and you will need your sales supervisor or officer to intercede for you.

Conflict and Competition with Fellow Salespeople. Sometimes there may be a salesperson who is threatened by your presence or your success. Although it is unlikely that one of these people will let the air out of your tires some late Monday night after work, it is possible that individuals may go out of their way secretly to sabotage your success at work. They may steal your accounts, bad-mouth you to management, give you wrong information, lead you astray, and any number of subversive tactics. Keep your eyes and ears open; learn as much as you can as quickly as you can; don't get caught playing political games. By all means, when someone proves to be an adversary, be careful about what information you share with him or her. Be the bigger person, and avoid taking sides in any political squabble. Just keep your eye on the ball, and do what you are paid to do without getting immersed in all of the nonsense on the side.

> ## Think About It
> • • •
> Favorable first impressions can improve your ability to sell more. You don't get a second chance to make a good first impression.

Spit-Shining Your Image

How you carry yourself and the image that people have of you can go a long way in affecting how they treat you and whether or not they drag you into the rumors and hair-pulling mentioned above. We've all heard the saying, "You never get a second chance to make a first impression." And think about it: Every day in sales you are making a first impression on someone. Although image may or may not be everything, it certainly counts for a lot. So what is image? A lot of things.

How You Dress. Many organizations today are becoming more casual in their dress code. I suggest that regardless of what your company's dress code is, always err on the conservative side. If you can't afford $1,000 suits and $400 shoes, that's okay. Just make sure what you do buy always looks professional, neat, clean, and appropriate for the prospect you are calling on.

Talk Isn't Cheap. What comes out of your mouth plays a big part in how you are perceived. We've all heard someone who curses like a sailor without hesitation. What is your perception of such a person? Avoid profanity, off-color jokes, snide remarks, sexist comments, political arguments, religious discussions, bad-mouthing, racist remarks, invalidating anyone, dealing in rumors, negative nationality comments, and lying—not even little ones.

Your Work Ethic and Style. Be serious about your new job, but have fun, too. Get to work early and leave late. And keep busy in between with productive activities, such as learning your product and service, studying up on your industry and your competitors, reviewing your organization's policies and procedures, understanding the marketplace, and establishing who the players in your industry. I also highly recommend you spend at least one day a month in the library researching your prospects' and clients' industries.

Your Performance. You will be judged in your first year not only on your results, but on the habits you develop, the routines you follow, the activities you engage in, and the lessons you learn. You will experience failure, rejection, and disappointment—guaranteed. Embrace it, accept it, and learn from it. No one likes a complainer, a whiner, or someone who always plays the role of victim. None of these are attractive, and none further your career—they might have the opposite effect. You will be observed to see how you handle these difficult emotional circumstances. The best policy is to understand that as you are learning, you will make mistakes, lots of them, so relax and learn everything you can from them. Napoleon Hill, in *Think and Grow Rich*, wrote:

You will experience failure, rejection, and disappointment—guaranteed. Embrace it, accept it, and learn from it.

> Every adversity, every setback, every failure, every problem carries within it the seed of an equivalent or greater benefit. So look for it, uncover it, and then learn from it.

Great advice from one of the great minds of the twentieth century.

Who You Hang Out With. Be careful who you hang around—they influence how you feel, how you talk, what you believe, and how you perform. If you want to become an eagle, fly with the eagles, not the ducks. If you want to be successful, spend your time with the people in your organization who are successful and soak in everything you can. You don't have to mimic them; just learn to pick and choose what they do that fits with your personality, philosophy, goals, and lifestyle. Travel with losers, and you will learn how to lose. Travel with winners, and you will learn how to win. This isn't rocket science, folks.

How to Become a Pro

Now you know what it takes, but how do you get there, step by step? There are many things and ways to jump-start and begin a career that are unique to the particular job and company. At the same time, though, there is a definite foundation you need to become a bona fide sales professional. Read on and learn.

Network

There is an old cliché that says: "It isn't what you know, but who you know." To help develop your sales career, I would like to comment briefly on this concept. I don't believe it tells the entire story. There are three other ideas I would like you to consider:

- Success isn't who you know, but who knows about you.
- Success is about who knows you and what you know.
- Success is about who you know, who knows about you, and what you know.

I have come to believe that you can know a lot of people, but if they don't know a great deal about you, the value of these contacts is limited. One of the keys to effective networking is the ability to both accumulate a variety of contacts in your database and make sure these people are aware of your skills, abilities, interests, and needs.

Think About It

• • •

It isn't who you know in life that is important to your sales success, but who knows you.

I have met tens of thousands of people in my career, but I would venture a guess that fewer than 500 can contribute to my success in some way by being able to introduce me to others who might be potential clients for me.

Networking Basics

Networking is finding people who may be able to be centers of influence for you, taking the opportunity to get to know them, and giving them the opportunity to get to know you.

Most salespeople are very poor networkers. They fail to join organizations where people who could benefit them congregate, or if they do belong, they fail to get involved or even participate in various meetings and networking opportunities.

How are your networking skills? Do you promote yourself with regularity in areas where influential people mingle? Do you belong to industry associations? Do you attend some of their meetings? Do you keep a database of contacts, where you met them, and how they might be of value to you? Do you have some system to keep in touch with them, like a newsletter, periodic notes, telephone calls, or e-mail? Who have you met in the past five years that you have lost touch with who could be of some value in your new sales career?

Be Professional

Selling is not what you sell, but how you sell what you sell. How are you doing when it comes to being a pro? How do your clients or customers think you are doing? How do you think your competitors think you are doing? How does the marketplace think you are doing? Don't wait for the results to come in from these sources. If something needs fixing, fix it now.

Don't Get Stuck in Your Comfort Zone

Over time, it can become easy to get stuck in one of a number of comfort zones when it comes to: behavior, performance, techniques, or attitudes. Let's look at a few of the common ones that many salespeople fall prey to:

- Calling only on clients or customers who you like or who like you.

- Only selling the products or services you make the most money on, know the most about, or are the easiest to sell.
- Slowing down your sales activities at certain times of the month or year (sand bagging).
- Once you have exceeded your quota or manager's expectations, adjusting your performance accordingly.
- Only selling to certain types of buyers.
- Avoiding certain buyer personality types.
- Avoiding learning new applications of your products or services.
- Spending too much time with customers with whom you have a lot in common regardless of their purchasing potential.
- Having nonproductive routines that keep you away from the real role of a salesperson.
- Spending too much time in after-sales service issues that keep you from selling more to new prospects.

Now it is your turn. List some of the areas where you feel you are locked in a comfort zone of some type. After you have completed your personal list, answer the following:

- How long have you had this behavior or attitude?
- How is this attitude or behavior sabotaging your sales success?
- If continued, how will it impact your career (long term, short term)?
- Why haven't you done something about it?
- Have other people noticed or mentioned the pattern?
- What can you do to change this attitude or behavior?

Sales is not an easy profession. It isn't something you do because you can't do anything else or because you want to make some fast, easy money. The real success stories in sales over the years are those people who have forced themselves out of their comfort zones and refused to settle for the easy route. If you want to make an impact in this profession, help your clients, and make an exceptional income in the process, you must leave the comfort of what you know from time to time and venture out into the unknown. You must take, as the poet Robert Frost said, the "road less traveled."

Get Out of the Box

Getting a fast start out of the box in your new career is one of the best ways to ensure a successful sales year. Many salespeople get lulled into a relaxed state as they begin their new career. Why not get an edge on your competitors before it is too late?

Pour it on. Make the first days as productive as possible. The quick-start concept discussed in chapter 1 is a valid way to ensure a great month as well as a great beginning of your new career. It is called momentum. Don't wait. Do it now.

To accomplish this great year, you have to be prepared. You have to plan. You have to be ready. And when is the best time to get ready? Now. If you wait you may lose. *Go for it.* Today. You will be glad you did. You have nothing to lose and everything to gain by using the quick-start approach to your new sales career. You may even surprise yourself as well as surprising your boss. Wouldn't that be a kicker?

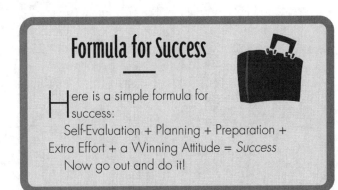

Formula for Success

Here is a simple formula for success:

Self-Evaluation + Planning + Preparation + Extra Effort + a Winning Attitude = *Success*

Now go out and do it!

Avoid Soothsayers

Sooner or later, someone is going to cross your sales path and attempt to discourage you, dissuade you, or even sabotage you. These people can take many roles in your life. They can be spouses, parents, friends, in-laws, supervisors, children, neighbors, or associates.

Tune them out and keep your eyes on the road. Don't give them any room in your consciousness. Forget the notions of: I'll try; another day; if I am lucky; if I meet the right people; when I have enough money; belong to the right groups or clubs; if I go to the right schools; had the right parents; was the right age, color, or sex; I am too old or too young, too short or too tall; too beautiful or too ugly.

Who are your soothsayers? They can be easily recognized. They seldom encourage you, pat you on the back, support you, or believe in you.

Get them out of your life, if not physically, then mentally and emotionally.

Get Real

People often say, "I just want you to be realistic." Being realistic is often an excuse for being negative. Or, "I don't want you to be hurt, disappointed, or to fail." Tune them out. Don't give them any room. Avoid them. Don't let them influence your dreams, desires, or life destiny. Let them worry about their own lives.

I have met a few of these people in my sales career from time to time, and I am sorry that I did not earlier recognize them for what they were. If I had, I would have saved myself a great deal of grief, while at the same time, accomplished more sooner rather than later. Oh well, later is better than not at all.

I love the quote by the late tennis great Arthur Ashe, "True greatness is, start where you are, use what you have, and do what you can." That says it all.

Learn How to Bounce Back from Adversity

Everyone, at least once in his or her life, experiences some form of a setback, adversity, failure, or loss in at least one area of their life. Adversity can strike with or without notice. It can hit a relationship, a loved one, a career, your business, your health, or your financial status.

No matter where or when adversity hits, the anxiety, stress, frustration, disappointment, fear, sadness, and panic leave the same feelings or emotions in its wake—a sense of hopelessness and despair.

Life is circular, not linear. First there is birth, then growth, then maturity, then death, followed again by birth or re-birth (depending on your beliefs), and so on. This is the law of the universe, whether it is applied to life itself or a change in career or a relationship. I do not mean to imply that all relationships must die before their time, but they do eventually end. There is a big difference. Endings are different than death. Death is certainly an ending, but there are literally thousands of types of endings.

Periods of life end. For example, youth ends and is followed by adulthood. All careers end, if not by premature death or a decision to abandon a career, then via retirement or the beginning of a new or different career. Relationships end. Their physical aspect—lust, infatuation—may end, but replaced with long-standing relationships with deep and abiding love.

Setbacks and adversity are often signals that some aspect of life has come to an end or needs to come to an end. They are wake-up calls, or what I call choice points in life. Many people, myself included on a number of occasions, have resisted endings for various reasons. Sometimes, however, we embrace or encourage them. We want to continue life, business, or a way of life forever. Most people die with unfinished business left in them. It is seldom that there isn't something more that could have been said, done, seen, learned, or shared by someone who has passed on.

Bouncing back from an event—such as a lost sale or lost client— is vital for your success, whether it was out of your control or you brought it into your life because of your attitudes, decisions, behaviors, or actions. What gives adversity its power over emotions, feelings, and responses? Why is adversity a tool used by some to improve or change, while others use it as an excuse or reason to give up, or to whine and bemoan their circumstances? Where is the potential learning or lesson in a setback or adverse situation?

Think About It

♦ ♦ ♦

Adversity and problems are normal. Successful salespeople use them as learning tools.

Fair Versus Unfair

Life isn't fair, and it isn't unfair. It just *is*. Life is neutral. It brings each person unique opportunities to learn and grow as a result of the events or circumstances that cross one's path. Everyone, I repeat, *everyone*, regardless of age, sex, nationality, religion, career status, or financial position, is a student of life. Some people, upon an outward-in first glance, may have it made. But do not judge by appearances only. Everyone has inner battles of one kind or another that they are fighting.

No one is immune to the teachings of life. Class is always in session. School is never out. There are no vacations. We never graduate. We don't get to select the curriculum, but we do get to do all the assignments and take all the quizzes. If we pass, we get to move on to other, sometimes bigger or higher, lessons. If we fail, we get to repeat the same lesson again and again until we finally learn whatever it is we need to learn as we travel through life. The repeated lesson might present itself from a different client, career situation, or any number of new or different circumstances, but the lesson will be the same.

Many of us, by choosing to see ourselves as victims, bring repeated adversity of one kind or another into our lives. To see yourself as a

victim and fail to take the responsibility for your circumstances is to live in an inner-emotional world dominated by blame, guilt, and resentment. I once heard a
friend make the statement, "Why is this happening to
me again?" Yet there *was* a common denominator in all
of the repeated events: *him*.

No one is immune to the teachings of life. Class is always in session.

Adversity Is Opportunity

Adversity gives us the opportunity to do a number of things as we
move through our lives. Some of them are: reevaluate old life patterns that are not working; see ourselves more clearly as contributors;
develop new attitudes about life, relationships, money, people, work,
and the like; and observe how we handle the lessons we are given.

People have asked me why some people seem to have or attract
more adversity or failure, while others seem to glide through life with
wonderful relationships, stable financial lives, growing careers, lots of
friends, and excellent health. I don't know for sure why some people
seem to have more, do more, and become more, while others struggle
daily with the basics of life. But I do have a few ideas and will share
them with you as food for thought.

There is a law in the universe called the law of cause and effect.
There is another concept that states: Be careful what you ask for
because you will probably get it. Still another says: What you are
seeking is seeking you. There is a great quote from baseball legend
Yogi Berra, "Expecting different results from repeated behavior is a
mild form of insanity." Another of Yogi's zingers says, "Life deter-
mines who comes into your life; your attitudes and actions deter-
mines who stays."

As you can see from these various different perspectives, a great
deal of the adversity and loss in our lives is self-inflicted as a result of

our conscious actions, expectations, perceptions, and thoughts or our subconscious values, beliefs, judgments, and paradigms.

All behavior is the result of a person's consciousness. To attempt to change behavior without first changing consciousness is to invite failure, whether the problem is with eating habits, communication patterns, work ethics, or everything in between. The reason so many people fail at whatever behavior they attempt to change is because they try to change outside-in rather than inside-out.

What does this have to do with adversity and bouncing back in sales? Everything. Our state of mind is often fertile ground that attracts adversity into our lives. Our state of mind will determine how we will respond to or overcome the events that come to us. Our perceptions, or filters (how we see life), will determine our interpretation of whether something is adverse or not. Give twenty different people the same adverse event, and I guarantee that some will see it as negative, some will see it as positive, and some will see it as devastating. The event is the same; the interpretations are unique and personal.

When we are confronted with a situation, regardless of its nature, that we perceive as a threat to our comfort, security, sense of well-being, or the status quo, we tend to imagine the worst. Fear takes over. How will I survive alone? Will I make this sale? Will I ever find a new job or career that I will be successful in? Will I ever find another lasting, nurturing relationship? What will my life be like with only memories of the past? Am I destined to struggle my entire life? How can I ever get over this tremendous loss? There are others, but I am confident you see my point.

When we operate out of a consciousness of fear, we tend to lose our perspective. We don't

Think About It

◆ ◆ ◆

Failure and adversity are teachers on the highway of life. They test your resolve, commitment, and attitudes.

think right, see clearly, or feel safe. We therefore see ourselves as victims and so are out of control of our lives.

Adversity can be an emotional tool for positive change, just like any other. If we hear the wake-up call, we can listen carefully to what we believe it is trying to teach us. This takes awareness, courage, self-love, and patience. If we are too hard on ourselves and beat ourselves up thinking, I am such an idiot, I'll never get this right, or I deserve all this bad stuff, we will find it difficult to create the proper mind-set to change direction. Adversity needs to be looked at with precision, careful observation, and honest introspection. It needs to be seen as one of life's teachers, and not some villain that is out to get us or beat us down.

Having said all this, it is also important that we not let ourselves off the hook with justification or acceptance. It is vital to learn to become more comfortable with where we want to be or who we want to become, rather than where we are or who we are.

So a question you should ask yourself is: What kind of a student are you as you pass through the classes in life? Are you a willing learner, or are you resisting the teaching, and thus the opportunity for personal growth?

Boundaries and Limits of the Profession

Every profession has limits and boundaries. Sales is no different. Sales, however, has fewer limits than do most other professions. This is the one profession where you can truly determine your future destiny in terms of your income, lifestyle, relationships, and freedom. The key to this freedom is your effort, willingness to learn, and your resilience. This is one of the few professions where you will not be judged by the number of hours you work, but what you put into those

Conquering Adversity

Here are a few things you can do if you find yourself smack in the middle of a situation that is uncomfortable, challenging, or trying to teach you something—in other words, adversity:

- Try and keep the circumstances or situation in perspective. Will this be as big an issue in 100 years as it is today?
- Evaluate the situation in light of your entire life.
- Focus on what you have, not what you lost. This isn't any easy step when you are neck-deep in pain, sorrow, or grief, but continuing to focus on what no longer exists tends to keep you locked in the past and a state of "no positive action."

hours; not by what you know, but by how you use what you know; and not by who you know, but by how you cultivate those relationships to further your success.

All professions require intense study, mastery of certain skill sets, and the development of productive attitudes. Many professions require years of formal education and years of climbing the corporate ladder of success; many also require licenses. In sales, though, you can out-earn your peers and exceed your wildest dreams for financial success in your first year. All it takes is a willingness to work—not an eight-hour day and five-day week, but through extraordinary effort and persistence. Your boundaries are set only by your own thoughts and self-limitations. You are the only element that can prevent your ultimate success.

Limitations

There are a few limitations that you will want to become aware of as you begin your first year. These are:

- Do something—anything—to re-focus your thoughts, energy, or activities in a positive or more healthful direction. Remember that you can't change what has happened, but you can change the future. And you change your future in your present moments. You also create all of your memories, positive or negative, in your present moments.
- Keep in mind the concept that you don't always get to determine what comes into your life, but you always get the choice of how to react or respond to it.
- Dealing with loss and adversity of any kind is painful and difficult as long as you continue to remain focused on the loss or the problem. To use adversity as a positive teacher that has come lovingly into your life to help you overcome shortcomings, character defaults, or poor judgment is a sign of emotional maturity. To wallow indefinitely in the negative circumstance, failure, disappointment, or loss is to remain stuck and out of control. Life is neutral. It doesn't care how you react or respond to its teachings.

- Your geographic territory or assignment.
- Your organization's compensation philosophy.
- Your organization's attitudes about developing its employees.
- Your management's willingness to give you latitude in your approach to your sales activities.

Even though some of these may be out of your control, you can still control your success by remaining flexible, adaptable, and open to the changes that will naturally occur during your career.

One of the reasons many salespeople fail is their negative response or attitudes to circumstances, policies, and procedures that they can't control. Sooner or later, your philosophy, prejudices, expectations, and attitudes will be challenged by your coworkers, your manager, or your customers. It is vital that you learn from these situations and people, while at the same time, keeping a close guard on your emotions, reactions, and attitudes. Refuse to fall prey to negative rumors and people. Be rigid in your development as you learn, grow, and master the skills necessary for success. Refuse to let other people or circumstances bring you down and discourage you. In the end, all you have is your attitudes. And your attitudes will determine your destiny.

You are reading a book on sales written by someone who failed in his first sales position over thirty-five years ago. Success is the best revenge. I succeeded because I refused to give in to limitations in thinking, creativity, imagination, and actions. I have broken a lot of rules in the process, but playing it too safe is for people who do not want to reach the top of the mountain.

The Importance and Necessity of Leverage

As you read the below story, "Starting with Zero," realize that it has a happy ending. I went back into the same business with a different company, and twelve months later, I was one of the top salespeople in the state in that industry. Several companies came to me and tried

Starting with Zero

Let me tell you about my first year in sales, over thirty-five years ago.

I was excited about the opportunity to become successful in a new career. I was willing to learn, work hard, and put the necessary time in to achieve the freedom that I desired. My employer, a major insurance company, hired hundreds of salespeople each year. Some survived, and many did not. I was one of the ones who didn't. The cause: I expected my company to train me, to give me the necessary skills to achieve success. In the first six months I didn't sell anything. Nothing. After that, I was determined never again to put my destiny in the hands of my employer. Their limited resources had a direct negative impact on my to recruit me. You can't possibly imagine the offers I received. Thinking back, it was all due to leverage. When you are your organization's number-one salesperson, there won't be much you can ask for that you won't get. Why? Leverage. If you are at the bottom of the list of salespeople in terms of your performance, I challenge you to walk into your boss's office and tell him or her you are taking the afternoon off! Never going to happen. However, if you are producing more than anyone else on the sales team, you can simply walk in and say, "I am taking the rest of the week off," and I guarantee you won't get much resistance.

So, how do you get this leverage? It's really quite simple—succeed, do well, be number one, and you will be amazed at how much freedom you will have, how much support you will get from other departments, and how little resistance you will get for most of your reasonable requests. Work on getting leverage during your first year and continue with a high performance, and you will get to call the shots for years.

ability to learn and succeed. I turned over my success to their training budget and the ability of my manager to teach me. His abilities were limited, so his limitation became mine, or so I thought at the time.

What did I know? I was only twenty-four, and this was my first sales position. I had nothing to use as a benchmark or point of comparison for their approach to training and developing their salespeople. Unfortunately, my lack of sales experience, insight, maturity, business acumen, and awareness of what to expect both from my employer as well as from my prospects and the marketplace contributed to my demise. The point is, your success is up to you, not your organization's financial position, philosophical attitudes, and management abilities.

You Are Your Future

Each of us creates our future—one decision, moment, action, and thought at a time. Some people are creating futures filled with pain, loneliness, heartache, insecurity, resentment, guilt, and fear, while others are today carving out futures filled with joy, happiness, peace, love, and security. Why will some salespeople spend their years coping with negative circumstances while others spend them in comfort, growing, sharing, and learning? Here are a few thoughts to consider today as you move through the decisions and actions in your new career that will determine the quality of your life tomorrow:

- All decisions have consequences—some positive, some negative, some immediate, and some long term.
- To see yourself as a victim is to secretly wish that your present circumstances will continue.
- We become a lot like the people we are around; be careful with whom you surround yourself or let into your life on a regular basis.
- Habits, both mental and physical, are created by us, and then they re-create the new use in the future.
- You cannot escape the truth that each of us is responsible for our life and its future outcomes. Casting blame, anger, and resentment for or toward anyone or anything other than ourselves for our circumstances is to live in the fantasyland of denial and immaturity.
- If you do not spend adequate time planning for and moving toward the future you desire you will spend your future days in frustration and anxiety.
- Living without balance in the critical areas of your life—physical, mental, familial, spiritual, financial, social, and career or

business—is to set yourself up for disappointment, frustration, failure, stress, and any number of negative conditions in some area of your life in the future.

Rediscover Yourself

This is the age of rediscovery.

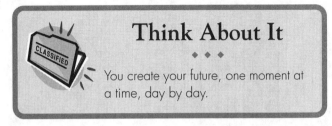

Bookstores are filled with hundreds of books on how to rediscover your childhood, relationships, sense of balance, your mission or purpose in life, and meaning in your career or business. Everywhere I look, I see people who are working harder at trying to have fun and find a sense of meaning in their jobs and in their lives in general. Is this an idea whose time has come, or is it the accumulation of years of searching and chasing after the empty values in life?

People by the tens of thousands are leaving corporate America in search of freedom, fulfillment, and a sense of control over their lives. People are leaving relationships by the millions in search of something more or better—whatever more or better means to them.

There is increasing evidence that many of these people, in spite of their renewed search for more, are still leading lives of "quiet desperation," as Henry David Thoreau noted. This was true when Thoreau wrote it, and it is still true today. Despite an increasing number of choices of careers, playthings, people, activities, travel, and interests, *frustration* seems to still be the word of the day.

What Is Rediscovering Yourself?

Discover is to obtain sight or knowledge of for the first time. To make known or visible. To expose. Not being an expert in linguistics, I

Cruising Through Life— or Not

I have a client in the cruise business. I recently spent three weeks cruising the Caribbean while I was working with the crews. I know it was tough duty, but someone had to do it. I had a lot of free time to observe a wide variety of passengers and their behavior.

People would push and shove to get on board the ship before it left port, and they shoved and pushed just as much to get off the ship when the cruise was over. I watched as people everywhere brought with them on board more than bathing suits and healthy appetites. I watched as they brought their relationship frustrations and agendas, their fears and prejudices, their anger and their hopes, their unmet needs and their attitudes about everything, both positive and negative.

One would have thought that these people, because they were on vacation, would have been able to relax and enjoy life at least for a week. Not so. If they were unhappy on shore, they were just as unhappy on board. If they were angry on shore, they were just as angry on board. If they were happy on shore, they were just as happy on board.

would offer that rediscover would assume that some people had already found what they sought, and we, for whatever reason, need to do it again. I believe herein lies a part of the problem. Most people have never truly discovered themselves the first time, so they are really embarking on an initial discovery.

To me, rediscovering means to experience an awakening of your true self; to feel those real feelings, fears, hopes, longings, and values that have shaped your life. Often because of self-expectations, other people's agendas for us, the rules of society, the rules of business, and the needs that we create due to decisions we make along life's path, we have built walls around ourselves to protect us from the world. What we have also done, uncaringly, is to protect ourselves from the real world inside—our own world. Few people really know themselves. And many who do, never achieve a state of authenticity or realness. Most people go through life on autopilot.

We have learned our reactions and lessons well. We play our parts with precision. And many of us have lost the childlike spontaneity and curiosity that are the benchmarks of peace and happiness.

I know, because I, too, have spent years building protective walls around myself. It has only been in the last few years that I have been willing to find the courage to be real. I must admit that I have a long way to go, but at least I have begun.

There are risks in being real. There are times when rejection cannot be avoided. There are times when other's judgments will, if we let them, creep into our behavior. John Powell's book, *Why Am I Afraid to Tell You Who I Am*, is one of my favorites. In it, John talks about the value of vulnerability and the pitfalls of hiding. I wish I had read it years before I did. I am confident I would have had fewer years of guilt, disappointment, struggle, and pain as I worked on becoming a human being rather than a human doing. Note the subtle difference.

Find a Mentor

Do you have a mentor? Someone who believes in you, helps you in your new career, and is willing to take time to contribute to your personal and career growth? Mentors offer their:

- Experience.
- Knowledge and wisdom.
- Contacts.
- Time and energy.
- Insight and counsel as well as compassion, understanding, and feedback.

A mentor can save you time, mistakes, money, energy, years, and effort. A mentor will not do it for you or make excuses for you. A mentor can accelerate your career, save you the trial-and-error approach, and generally add a wealth of experience to your cause, no matter what it might be.

A mentor can accelerate your career, save you the trial-and-error approach, and generally add a wealth of experience to your cause.

Over the years, I have had a number of mentors in my career. Each, in his or her own way, contributed something to my life, growth, and success. Some stayed with me for months or years, while others only served as my mentor for a short time. Each of us, as we grow, may become more, learn more, or accomplish more than our mentors. We may outgrow their ability to contribute to our lives. By the same token, some mentors may be with you for life. You might have less contact with them over the years, but when you do spend time with them, it will be invaluable.

I am currently a member of a mastermind mentor group called Master Speakers International. Our group is made up of eleven seasoned speaking and training veterans. We meet once a quarter to share ideas, get feedback, and generally brainstorm creative ways we can each build our businesses and careers. We have only been meeting for three years, but I can tell you that the ideas that have surfaced and the camaraderie I receive are priceless. I wouldn't miss one of our meetings.

Is there a group somewhere that you can get involved with that could be a mentor group? Is there someone out there who could help you by sharing time and wisdom with you? If not, why not start a group? That's the best way to surround yourself with like-minded people. It doesn't have to be a big group. A group is three. If you don't want to start a group, find someone you know who can contribute to your career in some way. Ask if he or she will be a mentor for you. I am currently a mentor for fifteen authors and speakers. It is a lot of fun, and they give to me as much, or more, than I give to them. Find a mentor and begin learning, growing from another's experience.

Create a Personal Mission Statement

The trend for the past several years is for organizations to run off to a secluded resort, hover around a conference table for hours, laboring over a mission statement. Why? What is the value? I must admit that I have spent hundreds of hours during the past few years working with clients to develop mission statements, vision statements, core belief statements, and the like.

The purpose of a mission statement, as I see it, is to develop a focused purpose and direction for an organization. Wouldn't this also be beneficial for a salesperson?

I have had a personal mission statement for years, and I'll be happy to share it with you: to learn as much as I can and share as much as I learn. This purpose has driven my career and life for over thirty-five years. A personal mission statement can:

- Help you through the rough times in your life.
- Keep you focused on what is really important.
- Determine who and what gets into your life and stays there.
- Give your life and career a sense of meaning.
- Help you wisely make critical decisions.
- Save you time and wasted effort.
- Help you have a more fulfilling and satisfying career and life.
- Live longer (I'm not sure about this one yet, but I hope so. Glad to see you're still with me).
- Reduce the stress in your life.
- Help you avoid career and life mistakes that drain your energy and creativity.

If you don't have one, why not get started developing one today in your new sales career?

Creating Positive Relationships

Make a sale, and you will make a living. Sell your client a positive relationship with you and your company, and you can make a fortune in sales.

Today, sales relationships are tested and strained in all senses—redefined with entirely new rules, expectations, and limits. As a result, the model of what makes a good sales professional is being radically modified.

These constant and increasing changes notwithstanding, managers are asking salespeople to increase sales volume and margins as well as improve customer loyalty and retention. This is no small order when you consider that, at the same time, budgets are decreasing, the number of support staff is dwindling, contact with management is declining, and expenditures for sales training are shrinking.

Whether you, as you set out in your first year of sales, are selling a service or a product, a high-ticket one-time item, or a low-cost consumable, I think I can safely assume that you are experiencing unprecedented shifts in consumer attitudes and purchasing procedures. Let's consider these issues:

1. Why and where sales relationships go sour.
2. Sources of conflict in sales relationships.
3. How to anticipate and satisfy cutomer or clients expectations.
4. How to manage conflict in your professional relationships.
5. Mastering the twelve steps to positive ongoing sales relationships.

Why and Where Sales Relationships Go Sour

Sales relationships that generally deteriorate share at least one of the following characteristics—in one or both parties:

1. Hidden agendas.
2. Personal agendas.
3. Out-of-control, inflated egos.
4. Unrealistic and uncommunicated expectations.
5. A lack of trust, respect, or both.
6. An unwillingness to agree to disagree.
7. Greed, selfishness, or both.
8. Ineffective patterns of communication or behavior.
9. Unethical behavior or lack of integrity.
10. Arrogance or ignorance.
11. Inconsistent standards or rules.

12. Unmanaged old baggage.
13. Inflexibility or uncompromising stance.
14. Clouded perceptions.
15. Critical or judgmental behavior.

Quite a list. Nevertheless, I've seen some sales relationships that have been affected by one—or many—of these factors and they survived. At the same time, I have witnessed situations in which only one of these factors put an abrupt end to the relationship.

The characteristics or history of a relationship can help it survive and even prosper, but equally important is the willingness and intent of both parties to continue working together. People will always have high expectations, jaded perceptions, issues of trust and respect, and other beliefs that can sink a sales relationship. Those will challenge the security of any relationship. I would like to quote one of my heroes, Will Rogers, who said, "There is no malice in my heart, so there isn't any in my gags. They are just jokes." If either you or your client has less than honorable intent or will, even the smallest error of judgment or miscommunicated item can alter the relationship. Everything that is a part of this relationship, regardless of its source or direction, will pass through what is essentially a new filter. Events that by themselves might not be relationship busters somehow become the final straw. And that final straw, like the one that breaks the camel's back, ends a relationship.

If the filter is not clogged with detritus, whatever passes through it maintains its integrity. This means that as long as you and your client want the relationship to work, you can manage any relationship issues or problems, whatever they are. For example, a shattered trust can be repaired, but you can't do it alone—it won't work if the other party brings other issues—old baggage, mistakes, and repeated misperceptions of trustworthiness. Your client must be willing to stay in the present. If their motive is to blame or manipulate rather than establish a mutually profitable relationship, then that agenda will sabotage any success at rebuilding trust.

Sources of Conflict in Sales Relationships

All relationships experience conflict from time to time. This is normal. Whether the relationship is one of three months old or twenty years old, conflicts will arise from time to time. A relationship that never has any conflict is most likely lacking in growth, passion, integrity, and awareness. But as a salesperson—as in life—your goal should not be to eliminate conflict, but to manage it.

Let's take a look at some of the common sources of conflicts in sales relationships—as indicated in the longer aforementioned list, there are lots, but these are some of the most important ones:

1. *Different personality styles.* Everyone is different. Each of us has distinctive likes, opinions, needs, feelings, attitudes, expectations, communication styles, and ideas. If everyone were alike, the world would be a very dull place. The benefit of different personalities is that some people can push our buttons, while others are able to motivate us to peak performance—to do our absolute best. Learn to accept that no personality is good or bad. We are all just different.

> *Each of us has distinctive likes, opinions, needs, feelings, attitudes, expectations, communication styles, and ideas.*

2. *Unrealized expectations.* Each of us comes to every relationship with expectations that are based on our previous experiences and desires. If we don't manage these expectations properly, they can

lead to a great deal of disappointment and frustration. Learn to communicate your expectations effectively while ensuring at the same time that you clearly understand the expectations that others have of you.

3. *Poor follow-through or follow-up.* One of the biggest sources of conflict in sales is when you make a commitment or promise to a prospect or customer and don't follow up. Here is my general rule for follow-up: Any time you do anything for a prospect or customer—follow up. Any time your prospect or customer does anything for you—follow up. Effective follow-up can take many forms. You can send an e-mail, make a telephone call, write a letter by hand, drop by for a visit, or send a fax. The idea is to make it clear to your customers and clients that you don't think of them only during your sales calls.

4. *Inconsistent messages.* Congruence is when what you say and what you do are consistent. Get in the habit of never committing to something if you are not sure you or your organization can do it. In other words, make sure that if you talk the talk, you can also walk the walk.

5. *Assumptions.* Assumptions happen when you are not communicating clearly with your client or prospect. Assumptions can range from a simple misunderstanding about a commitment to which you alluded, to a significant miscommunication about some aspect of the sales process, such as delivery arrangements, financial terms, quality expectations, or anything else that can be misunderstood. Remember—anything that can be misunderstood probably already has been by someone, at some time.

Whenever you get two people involved in a relationship where egos are in control, you are guaranteed to have conflict.

6. *Out-of-control or inflated egos*. The ego wants to control, manipulate, look successful, and be right. Whenever you have two people involved in a relationship where egos are in control, you are guaranteed to have conflict. The key to avoiding this type of conflict is to realize and accept that the world does not revolve around your opinions, experience, desires, needs, or expectations.

7. *Increased stress levels*. One of the major reasons that conflicts occur in relationships is that one or both parties are under a great deal of stress. People under stress tend to have short fuses, communicate poorly, jump to conclusions, be physically and mentally fatigued, lack patience, and have increased expectations.

8. *Hidden agendas*. A hidden agenda is when you want to say something to someone but don't because you want to avoid a conflict, or you don't want to hurt the person's feelings. Hidden agendas are part of every relationship to some degree. In a sales relationship, however, if your customer has a hidden agenda, you can lose a sale or even your best customer. How? They stop doing business with you for whatever reason, but they don't or won't tell you why. You just don't hear from them anymore, and then you discover—probably by chance—they are doing business with your competitor.

Let's look at the two major causes of conflict in relationships: personal issues and organizational issues.

Personal Issues

Why and how do personal issues contribute to conflict in sales relationships? Each person believes that he or she is right—whether the person admits it or not. The issue may be their opinion on how a product should be designed, priced, or distributed. Everyone sees the world as they think it is or should be, not as it is. People's views of a situation will always vary, even if only slightly. Inside issues such as expectations, assumptions, and perceptions are emotional issues that arise from thousands of sources—both internal and external. That people interpret things in various ways is what gives life its color—but also its conflicts. Life is full of paradox. Everything in life comes in pairs. Up/down, in/out, night/day, good/bad, and so on. If everyone saw all of life in exactly the same way, imagine how dull the human experience would be. So if we are to experience the joy of these differences, we must also learn to accept the challenge of the differences themselves.

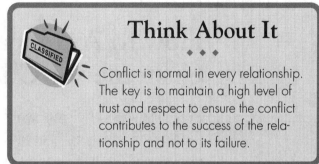

Think About It

◆ ◆ ◆

Conflict is normal in every relationship. The key is to maintain a high level of trust and respect to ensure the conflict contributes to the success of the relationship and not to its failure.

Personal issues give the participants the opportunity to grow, learn, modify, or adjust their beliefs or behavior as they get in touch with the source of these issues. Many people are attached to their own views and seldom are willing to see another or a different perspective. This single issue is the greatest internal cause of conflict.

Organizational Issues

Organizational issues are a little less personal and more a function of the organization, its culture, and its communication style. Let's take deadlines as an example. Whether a deadline is short or long is a function of several factors. First, who wants something done (the president or a file clerk, a minor customer or your biggest customer)? Second, what are the consequences if you miss the deadline (will your biggest customer have to shut down an entire division while waiting for your parts)? Third, how are you empowering your own people with the responsibility to get the job done. Fourth, what is the history you have established with this customer on meeting their deadlines? And finally, how realistic are the deadlines that you establish and under which you operate? Do you typically pad a deadline—that is, build in a little extra time—and does the customer, through experience, know it? Or are your deadlines realistic and well thought out?

How to Anticipate and Satisfy Customer or Client Expectations

Most customers or clients generally want the same things from their vendors or suppliers. They want a fair price; responsiveness to requests and problems; a friendly; comfortable sales climate; empathy for their needs and wants; people who are interested; and people who listen. They may want many other things as well, but most fall within these general areas.

Think About It

◆ ◆ ◆

Professional and effective after-sale service separates winners from losers in sales.

The secret to anticipating customer needs or problems is really quite simple. All you need to do is pay attention and integrate previous customer experience into your current actions, decisions, or behavior.

The buying public can, at times, be quite demanding, rude, and insensitive. It is important for you to realize that the behavior that people exhibit is often a cover for some other hidden emotional issue or need. For example, much anger is rooted in fear, and arrogance is the product of insecurity. When a customer is angry, you can choose to react to their anger, or you can look past it to try and determine what it is they are afraid of.

(Some anger, of course, may be fully justified, as when a salesperson fails to deliver what he or she promised.)

Successfully anticipating customer needs or expectations requires you to do various things. One is to listen; another is to be interested; a third is to see the situation from their point of view; a fourth is to show empathy and understanding. The fifth and final task is for you to effectively communicate your awareness, empathy, or understanding.

> *You can't always make every customer 100 percent happy all the time.*

You can't always make every customer 100 percent happy all the time. This is an unrealistic expectation on your part. What you can do is ensure that what you have suggested, recommended, solved, or anticipated is reasonable and acceptable to each client. Let me reiterate: You will never be able to satisfy or resolve every customer issue to that customer's complete satisfaction. The best you can hope for is to be reasonably successful with most people. Keep in mind that it is not always the solution or answer that is of primary importance to many people, but rather the manner in which you handle the situation.

How to Manage Conflict in Relationships

Again, conflict in relationships is normal. It is impossible to successfully anticipate all of people's opinions, judgments, prejudices, and expectations. Everyone sees life through the filter of his or her own experience and beliefs. Some people's filters allow them to have a more realistic view than others. Other people's filters are clouded with erroneous perceptions in the form of old baggage, unrealistic expectations and values, and beliefs that in no way resemble reality. You will discover that it is very difficult to manage conflict with these types of people.

Conflict results when two people have different points of view. You can use the conflict as a tool that will help either or both of the parties to grow. Or you can use it as a defense against modifying actions, beliefs, or behavior. Conflict is, in itself, really neutral. What makes it positive or negative is how you and the other party manage the source of the conflict. If you manage them in a positive way, you may both end up with better understanding and acceptance of the other's views. If you use it in a negative way, it can lead to greater stress, tension, mistrust, and, ultimately, the breakdown of the relationship.

You cannot change or manage other people's behavior. All you can do is modify your own.

To manage conflict, you must first look at your own expectations, agendas, and definition of what faults are. This will allow you to determine under what circumstances you are likely to become defensive, critical, or judgmental. Once you are in touch with these, your next step is to monitor your feelings, emotions, and reactions to other people's stuff (attitudes, perceptions, opinions, and the like).

If you find that certain behavior from the other person tends to "hook" you or "push" your buttons, what you must do first is to look back at yourself and ask why you are reacting this way. Why is what they are saying or doing affecting you the way it is? You cannot change or manage other people's behavior. All you can do is modify your own. You can't do that until you have a clearer picture of why you tend to react the way you do.

The answer to the question of how you can better manage conflict, then, is not to try to eliminate it. This will never happen. Sooner or later, something else will trigger a negative response from you. Learn to see conflict as a teacher, one that can instruct you about yourself and your tendencies. It takes two people or more to have conflict. If one of the two sees the source of conflict as an opportunity to learn, the negative dynamics of the situation can be quickly neutralized. As long as both people stay locked in an ego bat-tle for power, there will be no hope of a positive outcome.

Twelve Steps to Positive Ongoing Relationships

There are twelve steps you need to remember in your effort to culti-vate and maintain positive relationships with your clients. These are most important—the essentials, the foundation of any positive ongo-ing relationship.

People buy from people they trust, not people they like. The first step in building positive sales relationships is to ensure that all your words, actions, and behaviors contribute to building and maintain-ing trust. Honor your commitments. Don't make promises you can't keep. Follow through. Follow up.

Anticipate client problems and defuse them in advance. This can and must be done by planning, learning, communicating in a timely fashion, and understanding why the client views the situation as a problem.

Listen and read between the lines. Read the feelings and emotions behind the words. Have a sense as to what your clients feel about you, your product, and your overall relationship.

Be a resource for your client. Get past your selfish need to make a sale or earn a commission. Be ready and willing to offer your assis-tance, counsel, ideas, and support.

Build bridges, not barriers. Tell your clients what you can and will do, and do not tell them what you can't or are unwilling to do. Facilitate the relationship instead of complicating it.

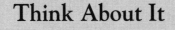

Think About It

· · ·

Avoid practicing your techniques and strategies on your best prospects. Practice with your peers, a manager, or friends.

Be your clients' ambassador within your organization. If you don't represent and relay your clients' needs and wants within your organization, who will?

Be a creative problem solver. Break the rules, push the edges, don't accept the status quo or outdated paradigms. Be solution oriented. Keep your clients' ever-changing needs and wishes in mind and work for ways to satisfy them.

Be available both when things are going well and when they aren't. Everybody loves sunshine and beautiful days, but how you handle yourself when the storms hit is what truly defines you. Be there through the worst of times as well as the best.

Know your clients' business, goals, culture, objectives, frustrations, needs, and desires. Study their industry and competitors, as well as the trends that have an impact on their business.

Create a team spirit, a spirit of cooperation. Achieve this between between your organization and your clients' organizations.

Be willing to learn from failure, mistakes, and adversity. You will learn much more from these than from your successes. Use them to refine your philosophy, strategies, attitudes, and approaches.

Understand that relationships are either getting better or worse. They are dynamic, not stagnant. Monitor the progress and dynamics of the relationship to be sure that you are in touch with its issues, potential, and progress.

Sales relationships, when managed in a positive and mutually beneficial way, can be rewarding for everyone involved. Your future success in sales will hinge on your ability to develop, build, maintain, and manage all of the relationships that affect your career.

Benefits of Positive Relationships

It is impossible to sell successfully today, for the long term, without developing and maintaining positive relationships with your clients. There are many benefits to successful sales relationships and success in sales. Here are just a few:

Repeat business. It is easier, less stressful, less time-consuming, and less costly to sell more to a present customer than it is to focus only on selling to new customers. The average cost of a sales call today is more than $400. Add to that the cost of acquiring a new customer, and you can easily reach a figure ten times that size. When you have a solid relationship with a client, they will tend to want to give you more business.

Making mistakes. Positive relationships allow you to make mistakes. Sooner or later, every organization makes a mistake; in shipping, manufacturing, finance, operations, or customer service. These mistakes are inevitable. If you miss a shipment date with a new customer, this can send them the message that they can't trust or count on you or your organization. When you miss a shipment date with a customer with whom you have been doing business with for several years, or even just a few months, they have learned that their interests and ultimate satisfaction are your primary concern. When mistakes occur, they don't become deal busters.

Price hikes. A good relationship with a client makes it easier for you to raise prices. Every organization has to raise prices. I have raised my fees every year for the past five years. My clients do not resist this rise for one reason: I have, over time, credibly established my high value to my clients. Unless your client perceives your high value, when you have to increase prices, eliminate a product line, or do anything that your client might perceive as negative, the customer will see no solid reason for continuing to do business with you.

> # Think About It
> ◆ ◆ ◆
> Remember—you don't do business in a vacuum. Your competitors are after your customers every day.

Referrals. Positive client relationships mean that you will get more and better referrals. One of the best sources of new business is referrals from your current customers. The longer a relationship, the better chance you have of getting a consistent flow of well-qualified referrals from them.

Learning. You will have the opportunity to learn more about your client's business. Your customer's business is changing every day. They have new demands from their customers, profit challenges, competitors, and constant changes in the marketplace and economy. The better your relationship with a client, the more you can learn about their business needs, issues, challenges, concerns, and opportunities.

Reduced stress. A good relationship is less stressful than a problematic one. Life is stressful. Business is stressful. Selling is stressful. Doing more business with current customers is one of the best ways to reduce the stress of uncertainty and relationship unknowns. Starting a new sales relationship can take a lot of time, work, effort, and creative thinking. Better to give all of this to a present client from whom the rewards are greater and more certain than with a new client.

Business growth. Strong relationships contribute to solid business growth. To increase your income, you have to sell more, improve margins, and reduce sales costs, all in a fixed territory. There is only one way! Maximize your sales results with your current customers while keeping your competitors at bay.

> *There is only one way to own the business—through trusting, successful, and mutually beneficial relationships.*

Less competition. You will competitor-proof the business. Your competitors want your customer's business, and they will do almost anything to get it. They will lie, misrepresent themselves, make outrageous promises, give stuff away, even buy the business. The only way you can keep the business in this kind of climate is to own the business. There is only one way to own the business—through trusting, successful, and mutually beneficial relationships.

Lower costs. You will have lower sales costs. Your turn—why?

Higher income. You will make more money. This should be self-explanatory by now.

Developing Positive Relationships with Your Coworkers

Your coworkers, regardless of their experience, tenure, or success, can contribute to your success. They represent the same products or services that you do, and all are experiencing similar outcomes based on their activities and attitudes. Cultivate these relationships. Be interested in them, both their personal lives and careers. You don't necessarily have to socialize with them, but develop the habit of sharing success stories, frustration, lessons learned, experiences, and needs. Use them as a resource for your development, but don't be selfish about it. Try to contribute to their success as well.

Everyone can contribute to your personal growth and success, even people who are not like you or don't agree with you.

You may have coworkers who, for whatever reason, you don't like, don't agree with, or don't relate to well. Fine. But remember, everyone can contribute to your personal growth and success, even people who are not like you or don't agree with you.

Selling Positive Relationships

Poor salespeople focus only on closing the sale. Successful salespeople focus on closing the sale and establishing the relationship. Which is your approach?

For many salespeople, the close of the sale typically comes at the end of the sales presentation. It represents for many, the final act in the sales process. It is unfortunate that these poorly informed or trained salespeople lack adequate understanding of the role of selling in today's competitive world.

Sales is not only about closing the current prospect on a particular product or service that solves one of their pressing problems, needs, or desires. It is about building a trusting relationship and partnership with them by becoming a resource, helping them solve their ongoing problems, and satisfying their continuing and evolving needs and desires.

Salespeople, for years, have been taught that to close a sale, they need to use devices or "closing techniques." For example, *"the which would you prefer, or get it before the price goes up"* closes. These techniques, although sometimes successful, tend to focus only on how the current product or service solves a prospects problem or satisfies a current need or want. The sales relationship must begin somewhere. The question is, how can you become a resource for a prospect, therefore beginning the relationship or partnership before you have sold or closed this sale?

First, you must evaluate your selling intent or the philosophy that underlies your approach to the sales process and how it affects both your ability to close this sale and the future relationship.

If your focus is on the short term rather than the long term, your intent is most likely only on moving products or services now. If your intent is to develop a long-term, mutually beneficial relationship with this new prospect, you may not close this deal, but that does not prevent you from beginning to build a positive relationship that can one day end in success.

It also depends on how you choose to define a successful sales relationship. All relationships, sales or otherwise, are dynamic. If a sales relationship is to improve, you need to pay constant attention to several areas. They are: trust, respect, acceptance, integrity, communication, intent, the relationship's direction, personal agendas, and a willingness to make the relationship work.

It is possible to begin to develop all of these with a prospect that you have not sold or "closed" yet. You can provide information, guidance, recommendations, solutions, feedback, and a variety of other services that would move the relationship from its current non-relationship status to one that is improving and moving forward.

I am not suggesting that you give away that which you sell. If you sell information or guidance, for example, don't give it away. That only weakens your ability to build a positive and successful win/win future relationship. But, if you sell widgets, for example, ask yourself, is there some other area in which you can help this prospect that strengthens your position in their eyes?

Giving to Receive

During the past twenty-plus years as a speaker and trainer, I have given away to clients and prospects hundreds of books and audiotapes by other speakers and authors. You might wonder why I would introduce a competitor to a client. Do I have brain damage?

No. This philosophy has served me well for years for multiple reasons. One, it shows the prospect or client that I am just as interested in their success as I am in my own success. Two, it communicates that I am secure enough in my own business and that I am not threatened by other potential resources that are available to them. Three, it shows them I am on

It takes more time, resources, and energy to generate a new customer than it does keep an existing one. It is also easier to do more business with a present customer than it is to find more new ones. What is your approach? Are you investing a greater proportion of your time and resources finding new business or on satisfying, developing, and keeping existing business? I agree that a continual flow of new business is the lifeblood of growth and success in sales; don't, however, make the mistake of underestimating your ability to use your present customers to help you with that mission.

Next, few customers will simply give you their business with no effort on your part. You must ask for it, but you also have to earn the right to get it. In my opinion, closing is more of a philosophy than a skill. It is more an attitude than a strategy. It is more about giving than getting, and it is more about service than your sales compensation.

What is a closing philosophy or attitude?

A closing attitude or philosophy says, "I am here to help you. I am here to do business with you. I am not on an educational crusade, nor am I a professional visitor." We all make the same income, regardless of what we sell, on the sales we don't close. Nothing. But the lookout for information or ideas that may or may not be related to what I do that can contribute to their long-term success.

In many instances, I have sent these materials to prospects before I have done any business with them. But in many more instances, this approach has helped me to distance myself from my competitors. Customers want value today. By showing an interest in them before closing the sale, I am creating the impression, "If Tim does this much before he has sold us, we can assume he will do as much or more after we buy from him." Granted, once I sell them, I have set up a high expectation for service and results, so I better work as hard to keep and develop the business as I did to get it. Otherwise, not only will I lose this business, but I'll also lose the potential of using them to get referral business or the right to use them as a reference.

successful salespeople leverage their time, energy, and resources by earning their customers' willingness to either directly sell new business for them or indirectly support their overall sales efforts with other potential customers.

Closing the sale or relationship is not something that begins at some magical point during the sales process. It is the attitude you bring to every good selling situation.

Costs of Poor Relationships

Poor relationships will cost you directly, indirectly, and every way in between. If you have a poor relationship with one customer, odds are he or she will pass that along to another customer. Here are a few examples of the problems caused by poor relationships:

Increased sales costs. Every new customer has an acquisition cost. This is what the company invests to make a sale, i.e., travel expenses, sales commissions, the cost of sales promotion materials, and so on. A new sale to an existing customer will have a lower sales acquisition cost than a new one.

Lost sales. When a customer has a poor relationship with the supplier, the customer becomes more vulnerable to the promises and commitments of the competition. As a result, customer loyalty can be difficult to maintain when there is a strain of any kind on the relationship.

Poor communication with your customer. Communication is the result of many factors in relationships. It is also an excellent benchmark to determine when a relationship is going well or may be in trouble. Poor communication between the customer and the supplier will lead to trouble.

Wasted time and sales effort. Spending time trying to salvage a lost relationship can be very frustrating as well as costly. Many salespeople attempt to save a relationship that is well beyond the saving point. As a result, they are not spending time with better prospects and customers.

Vulnerable to the competition. When a relationship lacks a positive history it seldom can stand the onslaught of aggressive competitors. They will say almost whatever it takes to ensure they steal the business from you. A weak relationship is a prime candidate for a competitor takeover.

Lack of customer loyalty. Most customers would prefer to do more business with their current vendor rather than starting a new relationship. When trust or respect leaves the existing relationship, customers may feel violated and will, without guilt, take their business elsewhere.

Increased customer pressure for lower prices and more benefits. When a relationship lacks mutual respect, integrity, trust, and understanding, a customer will tend to feel the need to be more aggressive in attempting to get lower prices. One reason for this is that nobody wants to feel that he or she is being taken advantage of.

Increased stress for you, your boss, and the organization. Whenever you lose a customer that your organization has invested in maintaining, there is naturally going to be a lot of frustration on the part of many people. This customer now has to be replaced, and the cost of acquiring a new customer is always going to be higher than in keeping one happy.

Uncertain business growth. Growing a business in any economy is difficult, costly and often frustrating. One of the best ways to build a solid growing organization is with repeat customers and referrals from them. Without a strong positive working relationship with your customers, you can't count on anything from day to day or customer to customer.

Your failure. Sooner or later, if you are not cultivating strong working relationships with your customers, you will find that you are always on the lookout for new business. Since often there is limited new business, you may find that you have no one else to sell so you will be looking for work elsewhere. New business is always necessary, but maintaining your current business is even more important.

Communication Is Critical

Communication in relationships is one of the biggest challenges today. Whenever you put two people together in a sales relationship, each brings different values, beliefs, expectations, history, education, agendas, goals, personality style, communication style, feelings, life outlook, and old baggage. It is difficult, at best, to communicate effectively with another person even without all of these differences. The key to better communication in a relationship is recognizing these differences and being willing to be flexible, accepting, understanding, and nonjudgmental of the other person's views, opinions, or communication style. Granted, this is not always an easy task.

Creating and Sustaining Positive Communication

This first step in improving communication with another person—if you are experiencing problems—is to look inward rather than outward for the cause of your communication difficulties. Since we all tend to "fall in love" with our own stuff, this is usually not easy. Most of us are doing the best we can with what we have at our disposal at the present time. Remember, when you judge another person, you are saying more about who you are than about who they are. You are defining your own prejudices and opinions when you choose to see the problem with another person as solely their fault.

Think About It

◆ ◆ ◆

Nonverbal messages are always more accurate than the verbal messages people send you.

Effective Communication Techniques

Meet people where they are emotionally before you try to take them where you want to take them.

One of the biggest mistakes people make in relationships in the area of communication is meeting people where they want to take them emotionally, rather than meeting them where they are emotionally.

Let me explain. Let's say a husband walks into the kitchen and says to his wife, "I am so upset. I thought Bill would have called me back by now. He is so irresponsible." She responds with, "Don't worry, honey, I am sure he will call soon." Seems like a simple and innocent enough remark, right? Wrong. The wife met her husband where she wanted to take him, which was that it would be okay; that Bill would call, regardless of her husband's feelings at the moment. But the husband was angry, frustrated, disappointed, whatever. She should have met him where he was emotionally and not where she wanted to take him.

The key rule of communication here is: *You have to meet a person where they are emotionally before you can take them where you want to take them.* The wife did not meet her husband where he was, but where she wanted to take him.

What could the wife have said to meet her husband where he was? "Honey, I know you feel frustrated and disappointed." Or she might have responded, "Honey, I can feel your frustration and disappointment; you have every right to feel that way (meeting him where he is) but it will be okay. I'm sure Bill will call soon." (taking him where she wants to take him).

Let me give you one more short example.

Your teenage son walks in the house after school, and says, "Well, I didn't make the baseball team." You respond with, "Don't worry, Tommy, there is always next year. It all works out for the best." Again, an innocent enough remark. Encouraging? Yes. Hopeful? Yes. Positive? Yes. But, it takes Tommy where you want to take him; that it will be okay in the future. But he is disappointed now—that is his principal emotion at the moment. You can't take people where you want to take them until you first meet them where they are.

Let's take another look at this example. In response to Tommy's remark, you say, "Tommy, I know how angry and frustrated you are (meeting him where he is). You worked very hard to make the team, but all your hard work will pay off when you try out again next year.

Don't lose faith; it will all work out" (taking him where you want to take him).

This same principle applies just as strongly whether you are dealing with employees, customers, friends, siblings, strangers, or vendors. This simple communication technique can dramatically improve the quality of your communication and your relationships.

Don't Invalidate Others

What is an invalidator? It is a person who puts other people down, insults them in public, disregards their opinions, does not listen, lets

Invalidators are everywhere: in homes, the classroom, the boardroom, on the golf course, and everywhere else.

their own ego try to control the other person, is emotionally manipulative, or negates others' feelings. Not a pretty picture, is it? Invalidators are everywhere: in homes, the classroom, the boardroom, on the golf course, and everywhere else. Where there are people, there are invalidators. I have had the fortune (and misfortune) to have had several invalidators in my life. It isn't fun, but you have a choice of how to deal with them. You can hide under a rock, lock yourself in the closet, fight back, give up, or run. I have done all of the above. How do you know if you work with (or for), live with, or just hang out with an invalidator? Invalidators:

1. Interrupt you a lot.
2. Ignore you or don't really care about your feelings.
3. Say things like: you should, you never, you always, you don't, you owe me.
4. Say "don't you"—rather than "do you."
5. Don't listen to you.
6. Are so wrapped up in themselves that for them, you don't really exist.

7. Are only concerned about their own needs and don't give a rip about yours.

8. Communicate things like: what will people think, you make me angry.

9. Also can be heard saying: How could you do that to me? See what you made me do! It is your fault; if you really loved me you would . . . . Why can't you be more like . . . . I expect you to . . . .

I could list a lot more characteristics, but I am sure that you can now identify if you are an invalidator or if you have one in your life.

Avoid Misunderstandings

Misunderstanding is a major cause of relationship stress, as are verbal confusion and improper interpretation of another person's motives, agendas, verbal content, and emotional meaning.

Some of the causes of misunderstanding are:

1. Hidden agendas.
2. Uncommunicated expectations.
3. Poor verbal skills.
4. Insecurity.
5. Poor self-esteem.
6. Emotional immaturity.
7. Wrongful intent.
8. Unrealistic expectations.
9. A conscious or unconscious desire to invalidate the other person.
10. A lack of desire to communicate effectively.

How do you deal with people who have these characteristics or simply avoid misunderstandings in the first place? Some of the following suggestions might help:

1. When you are unsure of the other person's meaning, ask them to clarify it.
2. When you feel misunderstood, ask the other person to explain what they think you meant.
3. Keep an open mind while listening to the other person.
4. Hold off on your judgments, personal opinions, and expectations while listening to the other person.
5. Try to make increased eye contact while the other person is speaking.
6. If you don't understand something, ask them.
7. Observe the nonverbal messages behind the content.
8. Listen for feelings as well as words.
9. Stay in the present moment.
10. Control distractions that may interfere with the message.

Misunderstandings do not need to take as great a toll on sales relationships as they do. If both parties will share the responsibility for the message—its accurate delivery and receipt—you can dramatically reduce the stress, anxiety, and frustration that you experience from communication problems.

When You Make a Point, Follow It with an Example, Story, or Illustration

We have lost storytelling as a sales tool in selling today. Years ago, the most effective salespeople were good (honest) storytellers. People need an anchor to understand your sales points. One of the best ways to accomplish this is by giving examples (choose ones that they can relate to) to help them understand your points. Let me give you an example.

I recently spoke to an audience of more than 500 salespeople. Half the audience was older than forty-five, and the other half was under thirty. Whenever I used an example to relate a point that the over-forty-five crowd (baby boomers) could relate to, I watched as the other half (the X and Y Generation folks) looked at each other blankly. They were asking themselves, "What does he mean by that? I don't get it." At the same time, the boomers were shaking their heads in agreement and smiling. They got it. When I made a point and related it to the under-thirty group, they smiled and said "Right-on," while I got the same blank stares from the boomers.

Years ago the most effective salespeople were good (honest) storytellers.

People Always Think That They Are Right

Keep in mind that people are least responsive to your idea, opinion, or information right after they have given you their opinion, idea, or information. They tend to relate to, understand, and even fall in love with their own opinions. When someone offers an opinion: "I think this is the best way to handle this problem," and you immediately respond by saying something like, "I think this would be a better solution," you send the message that you are not listening, don't care, or are not interested. Whenever anyone offers an idea or opinion, always ask him or her a probing question before you offer your response. We are not talking about agreement here, just sending the message: "I am not invalidating your idea or opinion."

Polish Your Vocabulary

The tools of the professional salesperson are words. We paint word pictures, we tell stories, we describe product or service features and

Think About It

◆ ◆ ◆

If you don't improve your vocabulary, you can't expect to express yourself accurately in any situation.

benefits, we influence, we inspire, and we hope to convince people of the benefits of doing business with us. All of this requires a command of language.

It amazes me how many salespeople have poor vocabularies. These people fail to realize that they are limiting their success, negatively impacting their destiny and lifestyle because they lack the ability to use the right word at the right time in any communication situation.

The key is having a good enough vocabulary to be able to effectively communicate with people of all demographics. In all cases, you need to be able to use effective words that your prospect or customer can understand. The ability to articulate your feelings, attitudes, needs, skills, desires, and knowledge is one of the most important ingredients for success in sales and in life.

How is your vocabulary? Do you often find you overuse certain words because you don't know any words that mean the same thing? Do you ever find yourself searching for just the right word for a particular situation? Is your poor vocabulary getting in the way of your future success? Do you tend to overuse profanity?

I have listed some ways for you to improve your vocabulary in the sidebar on page 117. Take a few minutes and list an equal number of ways (or more) that you can think of to improve your ability to use words and so increase your chances for success in life. If you really try, I'll bet that you can come up with at least a dozen that you could put into practice immediately.

Talk Smart

Your ability to effectively influence and persuade your prospects and/or customers depends entirely on your ability to communicate effectively. Yes, sometimes having a product to demonstrate, the ability to use third-party references, and the use of proof sources (articles, case studies, letters of reference, brochures, news stories, and the like) can help you achieve sales success. I believe, however, that your single strongest tool and skill is your ability to use language—words—effectively and correctly when selling to your prospects and customers.

Over the years I have seen hundreds of salespeople who represented a variety of organizations and sold both services and tangible products lose sales and customers because of their inability to articulate concepts, ideas, and benefits professionally.

All of us have one thing in common: Regardless of what we sell, how long we have been selling, and whether we are succeeding or failing, we all use words to communicate. I do not mean to play down the importance of nonverbal communication—actually it makes up a very large percentage of the meaning of the messages we send and receive, but I can't overemphasize the importance of our words. I can think of various areas to cover, but I would like to focus on just one—how to prevent misunderstanding by using words that prevent the possibility of confusion.

As you read the following examples, see if you can determine my meaning:

Word Perfect

You can improve your vocabulary in many ways. One of the best is: *Read more.*

Here are a few others: do crossword puzzles, play Scrabble, read magazines, learn one new word a day—that's 365 new words every year. In five years, imagine what kind of a vocabulary you could have if you used that technique. When someone uses a word you are unfamiliar with, ask that person what it means. Get a daily calendar that gives you a new word a day. Find an audiocassette on vocabulary improvement and listen to it as you drive.

Improve your vocabulary—improve your life. Pretty simple.

1. Our product is *better* than our competitors'. (What is better, how much better?)
2. Our service will *exceed* your expectations. (How much, when, how?)
3. Our prices are *lower* than *everyone* else. (How much, everyone? All the time?)
4. We *guarantee* your satisfaction. (How, for how long?)
5. We have the *fastest* delivery in the industry. (How fast?)
6. We are the *best* in the world. (Best what? Best at what?)
7. We are the *only* company that can. (*Your turn.*)

In all of the above examples, you are setting yourself and your prospect up for disappointment, misunderstanding, confusion, and uncertainty. The way to avoid this possibility is to deal in specifics, not generalities; to deal in words that create clear mental pictures rather than clouded ones; and to clarify how the other person is interpreting your message by asking probing questions.

Effective Listening

Hearing and listening are two different skills. Hearing is a physical capacity. Listening is a mental one. The ears collect sound waves and send them to the brain for interpretation, which is hearing.

One of the biggest complaints many customers have is that people don't listen. Salespeople don't listen. Many kids don't listen. In some cases, their attention span is less than thirty seconds. Employees often don't listen; they have their own agendas, and they are thinking about them instead of listening. Some parents don't listen to their children because they are too busy, distracted, or simply not interested. Politicians don't listen.

Why don't people listen? Because:

1. They don't care about the other person.
2. They are more concerned with their own ideas or thoughts.
3. It takes too much work to listen, so they just fake it.
4. They don't know how to listen.
5. They think they are listening.
6. They have no interest in the subject.
7. Their ego (the need to manipulate, control, or look good) gets in the way of their listening.
8. They don't like the other person.
9. The other person's nonverbal communication style gets in the way.
10. They don't trust the other person.
11. They think that they know more about the subject than the person talking does.
12. They don't respect the other person.
13. They don't believe the other person.
14. They are preoccupied with their own stuff.

When your prospects and customers share their feelings, fears, wants, needs, dreams, frustrations, or whatever with you, they are looking for one of the following:

Think About It

• • •

In sales you will spend more than 50 percent of your communication time listening. Do it well.

1. They just want you to listen.
2. They want your honest feedback, opinions, or feelings.
3. They want you to agree with them.
4. They want you to disagree with them.
5. They want you to share your feelings, experiences, or attitudes with them.

Guess which one most people want most often and get the least?

If you guessed anything other than listening, you may find you are having some communication problems in a sales relationship.

Here are a few things to consider the next time your prospects and customers share their words, feelings, needs, concerns, and emotions with you.

1. You don't have to like the message to be willing to listen.
2. Listen for the central theme of the message, not only to the points they make.
3. Stay in the present moment. Don't rush ahead or get mentally stuck in old baggage.
4. Offer feedback to demonstrate that you are listening.
5. Ask questions when you don't understand something they say.
6. Don't offer your opinions unless they are solicited.
7. Make lots of eye contact.
8. Stay focused on the other person rather than on yourself.
9. Don't become impatient if they take verbal side trips while they are talking.
10. Don't rush them.
11. Recognize that some people are only looking for support or understanding, not your opinions
12. Resist the tendency to consider your response before they have finished speaking.

Remember, one of the greatest compliments you pay a person is

Listen to This

Listening takes place on two levels: the conscious and subconscious. When you listen to a person consciously, you are paying active attention to their words, intent, feelings, attitudes, and meaning. When you listen subconsciously you catch their words, but you may miss the subtleties of their intent and meaning.

the willingness to listen to them whether you like, agree with, or are interested in the subject. Learn to listen well, and you will be amazed at how your sales relationships improve.

Are you a good listener? One way to find out is to observe how often you interrupt others.

Nonverbal Communication Techniques

Everyone communicates on two levels. Verbally and nonverbally. Verbal communication, or our spoken words, represent a very small portion (less than 10 percent) of our overall message. People can lie, misrepresent, or mislead you with their words. Nonverbal language represents over 50 percent of our total message. Effectively reading nonverbal messages can dramatically improve your sales relationships as well as your sales results.

If you detect an inconsistency between the verbal message and the nonverbal message that you are getting from a prospect, I would advise you to pay more attention to the nonverbal message. The nonverbal

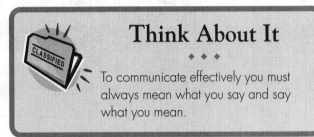

Think About It

• • •

To communicate effectively you must always mean what you say and say what you mean.

message will always be a more accurate representation of the person's feelings, attitudes, or beliefs.

We communicate nonverbally in multiple ways. We use gestures, facial expressions, eye movements and eye contact, posture and body position, verbal tone, inflection, pauses, pace, and volume. The way people dress also sends a nonverbal signal.

An easy way to determine what someone is thinking or feeling is to observe whether their signals are open or closed. Open signals represent acceptance, willingness, enthusiasm, and approval. Closed signals represent the opposite of all of these. Closed signals are crossed legs, arms, and hands. A lack of eye contact, rigid posture, leaning away from you and placing the hands on top of the head are also examples of closed signals. Open signals are exactly what they imply: open hands, uncrossed legs, eye contact, leaning forward, and so on.

I suggest you spend the next few days observing and trying to interpret people's nonverbal messages.

Getting Below the Truth Line

What do I mean when I say "getting below the truth line"?

Let's say your prospect says, "The price is too high." Is that really what they mean? How about, "I need to think this decision over." Are they really saying they need to think it over, or is there something more going on? How about, "I want to talk with some additional suppliers before I make my decision." All of these comments can have one thing in common. They are statements that the prospect makes that may not be the truth, or they may not be a reflection of what is really going on in their mind. How do you know?

You must learn to get beneath the truth line in every conversation or sales presentation. You must learn how to bring the real issues to the surface so that you can address them. If you don't, then you will not be dealing with the real objections or resistance. Traditional sales training asks you to use a variety of clever techniques to "overcome" these objections. I would rather you change your paradigm and see these statements and others like them not as sales objections but unanswered questions or concerns.

Let's go back to the previous three examples. What is the prospect really asking when they say the price is too high? Why should I pay so much? I can't afford it. I don't have good enough credit to buy it. Can I get it cheaper somewhere else? If I pay this much, will the product satisfy my needs or problems? You haven't convinced me it is worth what you are asking. How about the second one, "I need to think it over." What could they be asking or saying? I don't have the authority to make the decision myself. Should I get someone else involved in this decision? What if I buy it and it doesn't work; how will I look to my boss, customers etc? And, the last one, "I need to shop around." What could they be saying or asking? It's your turn. See if you can come up with your own answers.

A technique that I have used for more twenty-five years when I am getting information that I am not sure is true or is merely a cover for some other issue is, "In addition to that [whatever they told me] is there anything else that will get in the way of our doing business together?" I ask this for three reasons. First, in doing so, I am not challenging their opinion, view, or statement. Second, I am accepting whatever they are saying (not necessarily agreeing with them but accepting their words for the time being). Third, I am positioning myself to determine what else might be going on (below the truth line) that might stand in our way. Notice I put a trial close at the end of the question rather than simply asking the question?

The purpose of this is to send the message, "Tell me everything you have, now, that will prevent us from doing business together." I still have to successfully deal with all of these issues or questions to close the sale, but at least I know whether this will be possible. If I can, I have a sale and won't get a whole new list of issues after I deal with these.

The Importance of Mentors

One of the biggest mistakes I made in my early sales career was not immediately establishing mentor relationships. My assumption was that my employer would give me all of the tools, knowledge, and sales and career information I would need to be successful. I couldn't have been more naive. Yes, they did train me, and yes, they did give a certain amount of coaching, but I was soon to learn that every organization has its failings and shortcomings. There was so much more I needed to know and learn that I could never get from my company, managers, and fellow salespeople. Success requires more than knowledge; it also requires wisdom.

The difference between the two is significant. Knowledge is what you know, and wisdom is knowing what to use and when and how to use it. Every organization has limitations in its experience. None can know everything. Add to this the reality that the world is changing faster with every passing day, and what you learned yesterday could well be out of date, inappropriate, or even wrong today. You need a variety of resources and sources of information and experience to succeed and compete in this ever-changing world. In part, a mentor can teach you how to stay on top of your area.

Mentor Relationships

There are many career as well as personal advantages of having mentor relationships. But let me ask you a simple question before we get started: If you had the opportunity to cultivate relationships with people who could save you time, mistakes, and money, as well as accelerate your career progress, would you? Why?

Start Now

Several years ago I started a mastermind group called Master Speakers International.

Well, I hope I have learned all of the lessons I have needed to once and for all create a mentor group that can bring to my life, career, and business the ideas, feedback, support, love, interest, trust, and respect that I need to continue to grow. MSI members meet four days a year to share, evaluate, critique, and support each other. I have learned more in the last four years from this group than I have in the previous twenty-plus years as a full-time speaker. Why does it work? I have finally put all of the pieces together successfully. Don't wait more than thirty years, as I did, to find people who want you to help and who want your help. It can be just what your sales career needs to set new sales records year after year after year.

What Are Mentors?

Mentors are people who have an interest in contributing to your success, can add to your knowledge and understanding, are willing to help you, and put you in charge of what you do with the information or knowledge they share with you. They can also improve your results by sharing their experiences with you that may relate or contribute directly or indirectly to your efforts. Often, they are more successful than you are in some area of life, have already done what you are beginning to do, can be older (but it is not necessary), can be the same gender, but this is not a requirement. Many of my current mentors, and I have dozens of them, are females, and some are younger than I am.

If you had the opportunity to cultivate relationships with people who could save you time, mistakes, and money, as well as acceler- ate your career progress, would you? Why?

In turn, I am currently a mentor to a number of aspiring speakers and authors. Each of my mentees has different goals, agendas, experience levels, challenges, and needs. They also have other mentors, not only me. The more people you can get in your corner helping you, the better off you will be and the sooner you will succeed.

Types of Mentors

Mentors come in a variety of packages. They can be friends, rela- tives, business associates—or even a combination of these. They can be in a different career position; have similar or dissimilar back- grounds than yours; they can live near you, or they can live across the country. They can be less successful than you (depending on how you choose to define success). They can be retired, a former teacher, a previous supervisor, a distant uncle. Get the picture? Mentors can take many forms and come from varied backgrounds. What they have in common is their willingness to share their ideas, honest feed- back, positive and negative experiences, encouragement, criticism, out-of-the-box thinking, knowledge, and time.

Some can be in your life for a few months, while others may fill the role of mentor for years. This may sound a bit strange to some of you, but some of my mentors are people I have never met, and authors who died years ago, yet they share their insight and wisdom through their words that were written before I was even born. Wait a minute, Tim, you just said that one of the requirements for a mentor

Good Mentorship Gone Bad

Years ago I was in a business relationship with one of my mentors. I met Harry (fictitious name but a real person), and we had a great deal in common. He was a few years older than I was and more successful in business than I had been to date. We used to meet once a week to share ideas and goals. As our relationship grew, it became apparent that we had a great deal in common, but we also complemented each other's weaknesses. We began discussing the idea of going into a business together. We spent hours discussing business opportunities and our strengths and weaknesses and eventually decided to start a business together. For the first year, our relationship and mentoring grew successfully. But this relationship was now cluttered with the details of our shared business.

Over time we began to communicate less openly with each other. I stopped trusting him and he stopped respecting me. Well, you don't have to be a genius to figure the outcome. The relationship ended badly both personally and professionally. I have not seen Harry for years but I have spent time reflecting on where we went wrong. It was simple: a clash of egos. In the beginning, we were both willing to give up control, but over time, we became less so. I lost a good mentor, but more than that, I lost a good friend.

was that they gave you their time. What gives? How can someone who is dead share his time? There are different types of mentor relationships. Don't limit your thinking. Anyone who can help you grow by his or her insight and knowledge can fill the role of mentor. Some might call these people heroes. Call them what you want. I have a great many heroes who have departed this Earth who help me succeed every day. People like Mark Twain, Will Rogers, Norman Vincent Peale, George Burns, and many others. They help me daily because of their willingness while they were alive to put their thoughts, ideas, frustrations, encouragement, experiences, dreams, and fears on paper.

So as you read this chapter, think about people in your life—past, present, or future, from whom you could benefit. How can you benefit from people you haven't met yet or don't know? Create a list of skills, attitudes, and ideas you want to learn, and then find people who have those qualities. Whether you know them or not is of no significance. Don't let the fact that you travel in different circles from the people you eventually want help from prevent you from gaining from their knowledge and life experience.

The Role of Mentors and Mentees

Mentors play many roles while they are on your career team. Let's take a look at a few of their roles and/or responsibilities. Mentors:

- Are your best critics.
- Are your biggest fans.
- Play devil's advocate.
- Share ideas with you that you might not be in a position to learn otherwise.
- Are your best cheerleaders.
- Hold you accountable for your actions.
- Keep you in touch with reality.
- Help you avoid mistakes.
- Help you stretch your professional and personal limits.
- Help you learn new concepts.
- Keep you thinking straight.
- Give you new ideas or paradigms.
- Tell you the truth, even though you might not like it.
- Save you time.
- Expect a lot from you.
- Meet with you or talk with you regularly (or, if they are teaching you from their writings, you read them regularly).

- Introduce you to people or resources that can benefit you (perhaps in the form of other books, if they themselves are not around).

Quite a lot, wouldn't you say? This relationship is not a one-way street. To deserve all of this from them, you, too, have some responsibilities and roles in this relationship, such as to:

- Listen.
- Grow.
- Try new things.
- Be willing to let go of old habits, routines, attitudes.
- Ask questions.
- Be prepared each time you meet with or talk with them.
- Give them updates on your activities or results.
- Give something to them—don't just be the taker here.
- Learn new skills, attitudes, or behaviors.
- Do something with what they give you.
- Be honest with your communication.
- Not withhold information that would help them help you.
- Be appreciative for the gifts they give you and show it.

Seldom will you have a mutual relationship in which you will have all of the above from both the mentor and the mentee in the relationship. What I have described is the ideal set of circumstances or traits. This doesn't mean that you shouldn't try to find all of these, and be sure to give it your best to give all of them.

How to Select Mentors

The first thing I recommend before you begin to interview people to determine if they would be willing to be a mentor for you is to understand how you want to benefit from a mentor relationship. This may not be an easy task. How can you create a list of what you want to know or learn when you don't know what you need as you are beginning in this new career?

Following are a few things to consider as you begin to create your list of expectations, needs, and wants for the relationship.

Your reasons. Why do you want a mentor relationship? What are your expectations, agendas, needs, and desires? Decide what you hope to get out of a mentor relationship before you get into it. Explain to your potential mentors what your expectations are and discover whether or not your choices for mentors will be able to fulfill your needs.

What Mentors Expect from Mentees

Here are a few of the requirements I have with my mentees:

1. They must initiate the call or request for the meeting.
2. They must fax me, in advance, the question, need, challenge, or issue with which they want help.
3. They pay for the call.
4. As we end the call or meeting, they must put together a written action plan of things they will do with what I gave them or what we shared.
5. When they call or request another meeting in the future, we first discuss their actions from the previous meeting. If they haven't done anything with that information, I won't talk with them or meet with them until they have. They don't have to have been successful, only to have tried something.

Those are only a few. Every mentor relationship is unique. The purpose is for both of you to gain; the mentor by sharing and you by learning.

Your weaknesses. What are your weaknesses? Each of us is weak in some area of our skills, just as we have shortcomings in our attitudes. Before you can find mentors who can help you overcome these, you must be honest with yourself about what these are. Each of us has blind spots when it comes to our own weaknesses. To grow, you must get in touch with these.

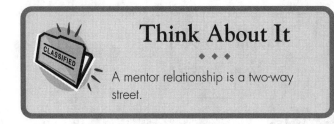

Think About It

◆ ◆ ◆

A mentor relationship is a two-way street.

Your expectations. What are the expectations of your new career that you lack experience or knowledge in? Any new career requires specific skills, attitudes, and knowledge. Your company or your manager may share these with you, but you may have to learn many of them on your own over time.

Your personality. Are you willing to let go of your ego and change your opinions and attitudes? If you are stuck, for whatever reason, in a set of beliefs, values, or attitudes that can sabotage your success, you must be willing to change them. Many people surround themselves only with people who mirror their beliefs and attitudes. The problem is, you all may be wrong. The ego wants to maintain control, look good, be right, and look successful. To change requires a willingness to be vulnerable, and to admit that you don't know everything—or even anything—about this new career and its requirements.

Over the years I have had many people in my sales seminars who had no intention of changing any behaviors or attitudes. All they did during the session was try and convince me or themselves that their ways were better or right, and that there was no need to change. I have often wondered why these people even bother to attend such programs. Why waste the time if you are in love with your own viewpoints? Have you ever read a book or listened to a speech, thinking, "They don't know what they are talking about. My way is better, or they are wrong." I know I have, and I also have learned over time that I missed numerous opportunities to grow. Looking back, if I had had a more open mind or more open disposition, I could have saved myself a lot of grief, time, and money.

Your goals. What do you want to learn or change? As you grow in this career you will need the benefit of others who have been there. Make a list of skills, contacts, ideas, solutions, needs—whatever, that you feel you need now. This list will change within the next year. Develop the habit of continuing to ask yourself, "Where am I now in this career, and what do I need to believe, feel, or do differently to succeed in the future?"

Your aims. What type of relationship would you like? Do you want to meet with someone regularly? Will you be satisfied to just talk with them once a week or month? Do you want them to be older or younger? The same or opposite sex?

Stick to Business

When I was single, I had a mentor relationship with a female fellow salesperson.

Years later, I had a proven track record. I was doing well in my sales career, but there was still a great deal I needed to learn. In the organization, the best salesperson was a woman. We were both single. She was bright, successful, and willing to share her experience and knowledge with me. Initially our relationship was strictly business, and I couldn't put a price on her advice and encouragement. Then it happened. We became involved personally, and the relationship changed. She was no longer a mentor. When the relationship ended, we both remained at the organization, but I had lost a valuable resource and mentor.

What went wrong? I should have known that sooner or later that a work-related relationship, if it failed, would have an impact on all other elements of the relationship. In hindsight, if I had it to do over again, I would have resisted the impulse to get involved personally, knowing that her friendship and mentorship was too valuable to lose.

Your contribution. What can you bring to the relationship? What have you learned or done? How can you help them? Understand and relay to your mentor what you bring to the table and how your relationship can be mutually beneficial.

Once you have created this list or answered the above questions, you are ready to take the next step. Don't rush through the

Good Mentorship Stayed Good

When I owned a franchise in the mid-1960s I had a wonderful relationship with a fellow franchise owner named Dave.

Owning my first business was a scary concept at best. I had invested thousands of dollars to buy a franchise in a business I knew nothing about. Looking back, I see that it was a good decision but made for the wrong reasons and at the wrong time. Needless to say I needed help; lots of help. I found the help I needed with a fellow franchise owner who had been in the business for several years and was consistently one of the top franchise success stories year after year. Dave and I became good friends. I trusted his advice, and he respected my willingness to learn. We were only a few years apart in age but had similar lifestyle desires. He was there; I wanted to get there. We would spend endless time on the phone. He would challenge my ideas, views, opinions, perceptions—you name it, he challenged it. He was also my biggest advocate and cheerleader. When I was successful, he was there with a big congratulations. I miss Dave, who died several years ago. But I will always be grateful and thankful for his insight, toughness, his holding me accountable, and his friendship.

Why do you think this relationship worked?

questions, though. If you answer them honestly, it can save you a lot of time.

The next step is to make a list of people who may fit the profile and who can give you what you need or want. Don't try to figure out whether they'd be willing to help you. Just make the list. Put as many people as you can on it. Don't limit it to people you know, are alive, live close, or any other variable.

Craft this list carefully. We are not looking for volume, but quality. Don't worry now about how you will meet or get to know the president of the nation's largest conglomerate; if that person fits your profile, put them on the list. I have many people who I would like to be my mentors that I haven't met yet. I may never meet them, and they may never become my mentors, but I have at least identified them and created a strategy to learn about them, get to know them, and get them to know who I am.

Start the Dialogue with Your Prospective Mentors

Next, determine which ones on your list would be the most beneficial to contact to begin the inquiry process. It makes no sense to spend months unsuccessfully trying to start a relationship with a potential mentor when there may be someone next door who could help you today. Create a list of ten potential mentors from your list that you can begin a dialogue with now. Tell them that you would like to meet with them to discuss the possibility of a mentor relationship. If they are receptive, start. If they are not, move to the next person on your list.

When you meet with them you will want to discuss your list of expectations and try to determine whether they are willing and able to help you. We are not talking about a lifetime commitment here—although you may get lucky and establish a lifetime relationship—only a short-term situation from which you both hope to benefit. Some words of caution: Don't complete these steps until you have finished reading this chapter. You might even want to wait until you have finished your first run through the entire book.

Notice I said *first* run through? To get any real value from this book, you should, I strongly recommend, read it several times.

How to Develop and Maintain Positive Mentor Relationships

Each party in the mentor relationship has expectations. The mentee seeks information, contacts, and knowledge. The mentor wants accountability, a willingness to learn and grow, and to use what they learn. To have a continuing mutually beneficial relationship, each

Politics and Mentorships

In my second sales position, I had an informal mentor relationship with one of the officers of the company I worked for.

I was working for a manufacturer in a sales development position. I had a lot to learn about the products, services, and markets of my employer, as well as about selling a high-ticket product. My first position was selling an intangible that was easy to understand and describe to customers. I just lost my passion for the business over time and decided to leave. When I began my new sales position, I was filled with optimism and hope. But at every turn, I was discouraged by how much I had to learn and how few people were available to help me. I befriended the senior VP of manufacturing. He was twenty-five years my senior but took an interest in me. We would meet informally once or twice a month to discuss how

person must have their needs or expectations satisfied. From personal experience, I can tell you that I have had no desire to continue to give my time and expertise to someone who is lazy, looking for the easy way, wants me to do all of the work for them, or fails to adhere to the rules we have established for the relationship. There are some things you can do to ensure that this relationship remains positive and mutually beneficial.

Ground rules. Establish the rules and expectations early in the relationship and keep the lines of communication open regarding these rules. If for any reason, personal or otherwise, you have to change them, break them, or ignore them, be sure to let your mentors know and why. Give them the benefit of the doubt. Keep in mind, they have entered into this relationship to help you. They are giving you their time and knowledge for free. Don't abuse this mentor relationship, or you may find you will lose a valuable resource that could contribute tremendously to your career growth and future success.

I was doing and what I needed to do to succeed. This was a wonderful relationship that lasted more than two years, and then something happened. He began to have difficulty with my direct manager.

I was between a rock and a hard place. I had to make a decision as to where my allegiance was. I chose my manager. That was perceived as a bad decision by the VP, and our relationship ended quite abruptly. As an aside, my career at that company also ended shortly after that. I am not implying that you can't have a mentor relationship with someone else in your organization. I am only cautioning you that these relationships have to be managed delicately. What went wrong? I was unable successfully to manage the politics in these relationships. I lacked the skill and finesse to be able to keep the one alive while the other was failing. As a result, I lost my job.

Time limits. Recognize that no relationship will last forever. Their agendas, needs, expectations, resources, and availability may change, and they may not be able to continue to give freely that which you have received in the past.

Honest communication. Don't play games with your mentors. They deserve better. Keep in mind, they have a life and possibly a career also. If you can't or won't do something, say so. If you don't have an answer or don't know something, admit it. If you want to end the relationship for whatever reason, tell them. Return phone calls, answer e-mails, and make these relationships a priority in your career.

Mutual benefits. Find ways to contribute to their success. Whether it is information you run across, books you have read, Web sites you have found that you feel might be of interest to them, customers you can bring to them, or problems you can help them solve, share these freely and openly with them on a timely basis.

Reap the Benefit of Another's Experience

My father has always been a powerful mentor in my life.

My father is now in his mid-eighties. He has been retired for more than twenty years, but I can tell you that every time I have a significant challenge or desire, big plan, or serious problem, he has been there with an unbiased attitude. I didn't always like what he had to say, but somehow, I knew I should pay attention—that some day his words of wisdom, counsel, or chastisement would come in handy. Not all of us are blessed with parents who have both the love and the knowledge to help us in our later years as life and business challenge us. I was one of the lucky ones. He gave me both, and still does. Keep in mind he knows nothing about the business of speaking and writing. A mentor doesn't have to know intimately what you do. They only have to be willing to give you their honest feedback and appraisal from their years of experience.

Trust counts. Maintain a high level of trust and respect. Every relationship, sooner or later, has conflict. This one will, too. If you have a high level of trust and respect, any conflict that you have due to different viewpoints, attitudes, or opinions will be resolved quickly and easily.

Show respect. Respect their time and knowledge. Your mentors may at times share valuable personal insights, values, beliefs, and philosophies with you. You don't have to agree with them, but you can learn from them.

Listen and learn. Recognize the challenges to a successful ongoing relationship. You are in a new career; you will be changing, learning, and growing every day. Your mentors may have already been where you are. When they offer counsel, advice, or feedback, it is most likely given with a positive and respectful agenda. Recognize that they are sharing what they believe you want or need. They may recognize this before you do. There is a great old saying that states: When the student is ready, the teacher appears. They may at times have insights that you are not ready for. Accept them and store them away for future review and consideration.

Think About It

• • •

To be successful, a mentor relationship must have rules and clearly expressed expectations.

Keep records. Start a mentor journal and record all of the ideas, information, insights, and questions you have received or asked, or those that you want to in the future. Write everything down for future review, evaluation, and consideration. I recommend a three ring binder. You can create tabs for:

- Expectations you have of them.
- Expectations they have of you.
- Questions to ask.
- Things you have learned.
- Things to share with them.
- Lessons you have learned.
- Changes you have made.
- Actions you will take.
- Results you have achieved.
- Thoughts you have had.
- Experiences you have had or want to share.
- Realizations you have come to.
- Views or opinions that you have changed.
- A history of your meetings and telephone conversations.

This is just a partial list. Keep only those items that you think are appropriate for you in this relationship. If you have more than one mentor relationship at a time, you can keep all of this in one binder; you don't have to have fourteen binders on your desk.

Don't Force It

Early in my speaking career, I started a mastermind group with a dozen other speakers.

Over the years I had the value of sharing ideas with like-minded people. I had also had a history of trying to develop mentor relationships that were win-win in their purpose and process. In the early part of my speaking and writing career, operating as a sole business owner, I knew I needed input, feedback, and ideas from other successful speakers and authors. So I invited a group of people in my business to form a mastermind group where we would share ideas, critique each other's materials, marketing plans, and products. From the beginning, it was clear that this group would not succeed. There were too many individual agendas and competing philosophies. We lasted for less than six months as a formal group. Each meeting was a struggle to accomplish anything worthwhile. I ended up wasting a great deal of time and money in this effort.

What went wrong? I was trying too hard to make the relationships work. A mentor relationship, if it is to be successful, must flow. It should be easy and have very little stress.

How Do You Know When the Relationship Is Working?

Well folks, we are in the home stretch. I hope that I have convinced you of the importance of establishing, maintaining, and learning from a mentor relationship. There are just a few other things I would like you to think about. How do you know when a relationship is working and how do you know when it isn't, and you should end it and move on?

There are warning signs when a relationship is not working, just as there are also signals that it is a positive and mutually beneficial one you should work on continuing. Notice I said work on? Mentor relationships are like any others: They take effort, commitment, energy, and time to develop and maintain. No relationship, if it is to be worthwhile, will come easy. You and your mentor are bound to disagree and have misunderstandings, conflicts, and personal agendas. These, however, do not have to cause the relationship to end.

If a relationship is working, it will generally be free of mistrust, stress, hidden agendas, unspoken expectations, unresolved conflicts, and old baggage. It will be respectful, helpful, encouraging, honest, and safe. If and when you lose any of these characteristics, it may be a sign that the relationship is coming to an end. If so, how do you know when it is time to move on?

There are several ways to tell if the relationship is no longer working. Here are a few of the common ones:

1. You have stopped communicating on a regular basis with your mentor (either because he or she has or you have).
2. You are now performing out of obligation or guilt rather than desire.
3. Trust, respect, or both are no longer part of the relationship.
4. Your mentor can no longer help you. Your needs and desires have outgrown this relationship. Keep in mind that just because the mentor relationship has ended, you can still maintain the friendship, if you had one.
5. Your mentor is too busy for you.
6. You have lost interest in this relationship.
7. It is becoming destructive and critical, rather than being supportive and positive.

I'll leave you with a question before we go on to chapter 6. What are you going to do with the information in this chapter?

The Greatest Challenges in Sales

6

Every profession has problems, challenges, opportunities, risks, and potential failures. No one is immune to these hazards, but everyone can benefit from the opportunities. If you pay close attention during your first year, you will notice that some of your peers will do exceedingly well with the tools, training, and opportunities that they are given. Others, in contrast, will misuse or not use these benefits at all. You will also become acutely aware of how some of your fellow salespeople fail or do poorly, while others chart a very successful financial course into the future. Why, if two people are given the same opportunities and products or services to sell, plus the same challenges, economy, management team, and risks, would one do well while others do poorly, or even fail?

I have asked myself this question over and over again during my thirty-plus years as a trainer. My conclusion is this: I don't know.

Remember, it always costs more to fail than to succeed in any area of life, and sales is no different.

However, there are a few symptoms, clues, and warning signs that I have observed and discovered that may help you avoid the catastrophe of failure. Remember, it always costs more to fail than to succeed in any area of life, and sales is no different.

Success Versus Failure

The price of success is a willingness to learn, work, grow, and persist. The cost of failure is enormous emotionally, financially, and physically. If you fail, consider what you are up against:

- You have to look for a new position.
- Your track record will make it harder to secure a favorable new position.
- You may have to move to a smaller residence, perhaps unloading some of your possessions. In the process, your personal relationships could be dramatically affected.
- Your self-esteem will take a beating.
- You will have to learn a new career or job.
- You may have to cultivate an entirely new group of friends and associates.

Although you might not experience all of these, you would certainly encounter some, as well as other unforeseen consequences. So it is best to avoid such catastrophic failure. Now we need to learn how to do that.

Pathway to Success

Your career, like most, will probably be riddled with potholes, missed opportunities, and mistakes. At the same time, you will also experience your share of opportunities to succeed. But to open life to the good, you need to learn how to deal with the bad. So let's look at some of the challenges you will inevitably face as your career develops and continues.

Life Versus Work Challenges

As we discussed previously, you will to learn to balance your new career and your personal life successfully. How best to handle that?

Maintaining balance is not easy in any career. It is especially difficult in the sales profession. Many people will want, need, or even demand your time. There are customers, suppliers, fellow salespeople, managers, and executives. Each of these groups has specific needs or desires for which you will be responsible.

Think About It
♦ ♦ ♦

Desire is the great equalizer. Your ability to maintain a high level of desire regardless of what is going on around you will greatly determine your success.

You will be required to be at your customers' beck and call and to travel to trade shows at the last minute. You will be required to attend seminars, company meetings, and briefings that can last well past normal working hours. There is no such thing as "normal" in sales. I have worked twenty-four-hour days and many seven-day weeks. You will have to work your personal vacation time and your other time off around client and management expectations.

How to Prepare for the Balancing Act

The key to effective balance, to preventing these demands from overwhelming your personal relationships and interests, is to keep everything in perspective. Remind yourself regularly that this field provides the income that allows you to live the way you choose, but it, in my opinion, should never totally dominate your life. Life is meant to be fun, rewarding, fulfilling, and challenging, but you do not need to derive all of these satisfactions from your career. It is important to love what you are doing so that you work the twenty-four-hour-days out of love rather than out of obligation or guilt. The day that the love of my profession dwindles so that I am no longer willing to spend several hours each week on planes so I can have the privilege of speaking to an audience, is the day both me and my audience will no longer benefit from my message.

Think About It

◆ ◆ ◆

Selling and life can be hard, and sooner or later, everyone wants to quit. But the key is to understand the difference between wanting to quit and actually quitting.

The day I stop enjoying spending long, quiet hours at my computer—sometimes into the early hours of the next morning—I will begin to wonder whether what I write will have any redeeming value for my readers or give me any real sense of satisfaction.

How to Manage the Balancing Act

The first thing you can do to manage this challenge is to accept that you will eventually have to address this career issue. At the same time, you'll need to recognize that that if you don't, it could have a seriously negative effect on your ultimate success in sales. What you need to recognize, really, is your ability to deal with reality and the natural career growth stages that you will experience. Depending on your age, relationship status, and emotional maturity as you begin your new sales career, you will encounter different challenges.

If you are in your twenties and single, your new career will most likely affect only your social life (although don't discount this—a lost social life may mean passing up future family happiness). However, if you are in your thirties or forties and married or divorced, you will confront an entire different set of problems; children, a spouse or ex-spouse, and numerous social and family obligations. The key to managing these challenges successfully is keeping the lines of communication open and being honest with those people to whom you are close. As your responsibilities in your personal relationships change, you will need to grow into those obligations with clarity, flexibility, and patience.

How to Prevent Falling Off the Tightrope

The Balancing Act

Balance is about love—loving what you do, whether it is work or play, being alone or with friends or family. Sooner or later you will have to make some hard choices. Should you have a family weekend or spend two days boning up on a new presentation? Should you leave work early to attend your six-year-old's birthday celebration or put the finishing touches on an important proposal? These choices will never be easy, but sooner or later, you'll have to make them anyway.

Balance is about goals. We have spent a great deal of time discussing the importance of goals. Again, without clear, focused, written, carefully thought-out goals, you will never enjoy real balance, harmony, and inner peace in your life. You will always feel as though, in some area of your life, you're being cheated, or it has spun out of control. You will add unnecessary stress to your life. When you come to that point, and you will, sooner or later, you will have to make some difficult choices. Better to have a road map that shows you why you decided what you did so that you can devote your full energy and total passion to what you are doing at the time.

In all honesty, I must say that you can't prevent your work obligations from affecting the rest of your life—and your career. This is true not only in sales, but in virtually all professions. Success means making tradeoffs. Life changes—get used to it. People change. Your desires, goals, and needs change. The best strategy is to remain aware that you will need to face these challenges—if not today, then tomorrow.

Handling Rejection

You must be able to emotionally handle the rejection that is inherent and natural in sales. We all want to be approved of, validated, and accepted. No one likes rejection, whether it comes from a friend, relative, total stranger, or fellow employee. The rejection that you will experience in your sales career is a normal element of the profession. Sooner or later, you will encounter a prospect or customer who doesn't like you, doesn't want to see you, or is even offended by your sales attempts or efforts to see them or sell them. And even if they like you, they simply may not need the product or service that you're selling at that particular time. It is impossible to expect that everyone you attempt to see or sell to is going to want to see you, be interested, or even curious about what you have to offer.

Think About It

◆ ◆ ◆

Anything worthwhile comes after you have overcome a challenge. If something comes to you without challenge, you won't give it much value or feel much satisfaction.

How to Prepare for the Inevitable Rejection

One of the biggest challenges you will face in your new career is the ability to effectively manage this rejection, which, if you are not careful, can make you feel discouraged, frustrated, and even like a failure. I have been studying sales success and failure for more than forty years, and I strongly believe that the inability to successfully deal with this challenge is the number-one cause of failure in sales. Why?

Each of us has a fundamental psychological need or desire to be liked. Each of us likes to be around people who agree with us and enjoy our company. We dislike spending time with people who are constantly pushing our emotional buttons or who we find unpleasant in their demeanor or philosophy. We have organized our lives to ensure that most of our time is spent in the presence of positive like-minded people, rather than those who are our emotional opposites. The best way to prepare for rejection is to accept that life is not a popularity contest; understand that not everyone you meet will like you—nor will you like them; and recognize that once you overcome this fear of rejection, you are well on your way to exceptional success in your new sales career.

How to Manage Rejection

You can take various approaches in dealing with this issue. Each will require some stretching, consideration, and willingness to set aside some of your current fears, expectations, and attitudes.

Talk with Strangers. First, you can start talking more to strangers, people you meet on street corners, in elevators, or in coffee shops. The key is to start a conversation with everyone you don't know by bringing up a general topic that fits the situation. Have you ever been here before? Is the coffee good? Have you ever tried the restaurant next door? Good morning. Hi. (These you might want to consider saying first).

Try *anything* that is nonthreatening. I have even used this tactic in New York City, a place where it is "against the law" to talk to strangers. You would be amazed how many people will see your attempt at idle conversation as an intrusion and how many people will welcome the opportunity to talk with someone. The point is to develop the habit of talking to strangers and getting used to the rejection you get from some people.

Recently I tried to start a conversation with a woman in an elevator in Washington, D.C., with a simple unobtrusive "Good morning." She responded, "Are you addressing me?" I said "Well, it's just you and I on this elevator and I usually don't say good morning to myself out loud." She said, "Do I know you?" I replied, "No." Just use your imagination a little and you can quickly guess where this conversation went—nowhere.

Cold Call. Second, spend fifteen minutes a day calling prospects who don't know you and may have never heard of your organization. You will tend to get blown off a lot if you don't have a good opening approach. Again, the point is to develop some emotional stamina in dealing with rejection.

Here's one more: Make three physical cold calls a day. While I am not advocating cold calling as an effective prospecting method, I am only suggesting it as a way of learning to cultivate the ability to not take rejection personally.

You can't prevent the possibility of rejection in your career. There is only one way to avoid or prevent rejection, and that's to never attempt to see people, sell to people, or ask for the business.

How to Prevent Rejection. You can't prevent the possibility of rejection in your career. There is only one way to avoid or prevent rejection, and that's to never attempt to see people, sell to people, or ask for the business. You will never experience rejection by staying in your office, car, or at your desk.

Forge Ahead

Essential for success is the ability to stick with it—whatever it may be—during long periods of poor results. You must be able to face your failures, put them aside, and keep battling for the results you desire.

How to Develop Persistence

One of the critical skills for success in sales is persistence, or what might be called, the stick-to-it quality. That may not be a word, but it gets the point across. Many people expect life and sales to be easy and to have immediate, positive results. One of the requirements for success in sales is the ability to get your prospect pipeline full and then keep it full with regular, consistent, professional prospecting. Nothing that is worthwhile ever comes easily or quickly—trust me, I know. If you expect immediate results, you will live with a great deal of frustration in your career.

How to Manage Persistence

Persistence is a habit that is formed over time. I won't go so far as to say that the ability to hang in there is in your physical genes; but if you have it as a trait, you have most likely exhibited it during your early childhood, education, or any task or activity that you have started in the past. You can develop this habit of persistence now if it is not part of your mental make-up, but you will need patience and, yes, persistence, to develop the habit of persistence. Seems like a paradox, doesn't it, learning to stick with things by sticking with things?

I am, by nature, a do-it-now persistent-type person in most areas of my life. I just refuse to quit. In fact, I have a sign over my desk that has been there for years that says, "You never fail—until you stop trying." Any success I have had thus far in my life and career has had little to do with my education, luck, or contacts. I have achieved it purely by my attitude that no matter what, I would never give in to failure,

Success Can Lead to Failure

I recall, over twenty years ago, working with a new client in the real estate business in Washington, D.C. One of the newer salespeople, she had only been working with the firm for a few weeks, made a sale of a new home in the half-million dollar price range in her second week as a part-time agent. She was feeling excited, confident, and almost arrogant. When I talked with her and said that I thought that this quick success was one of the worst things that could have happened to her in her new career, she was astonished. "Why?" she asked, with a little edge in her voice. I responded with the following.

"Sarah, long-term success in sales requires attitude management skills, effective prospecting, long, hard hours, learning to deal with rejection and disappointment, and knowing

discouragement, or challenges that appeared insurmountable. How have I been able to do this in the face of relentless problems, adversity, setbacks, and failures? It is simple for me; my mind contains no room for giving up. I just refuse to accept failure as final. It is only a detour.

I suggest that you learn persistence in the little things first. Get in the habit of having small successes. Then, build on these as you strengthen your resolve, confidence, and commitment. Why not keep a persistence log? Track all of those activities, projects, and tasks. How did you do? Did you quit early? If so, why? Did you stick with them to their conclusion? If so, why?

How to Prevent Negative Perseverance

I have learned that sooner or later, each of us will be brought to our knees in some area of our lives. The key to avoiding this is to not give any mental energy to anything other than your goals and how, why, and when you want to achieve them. If it takes your entire life, how to sell in different sales situations. Succeeding early, although I certainly congratulate you, was not the result of any of the previous factors. You were lucky. Now, luck is a good thing to have in life, but it won't guarantee your success if you develop the belief that this business is easy. What will your attitude be if you sell nothing for the next six months?"

"That won't happen to me," she responded. I could see I wasn't getting my point across, so I asked her one more question.

"Sarah, do you think all of your sales will be this easy, or come this quickly?" She responded with a confident, "Yes." Well, to make a very long story short, she failed to make her sales several weeks later. In fact, she never sold another home. She quit. She did not develop the skills and attitudes necessary for long-term success.

so be it. I have also learned that surrender, not giving up but letting life be, is an excellent way to live without the added stress that comes with yielding to discouragement and failure.

As we have discussed earlier, failure, risk, problems, and the like are a part of life, just as are success, achievement, and overcoming challenges. The thing to remember is that sooner or later, you are going to want to give up. This is fine. Just don't do it.

Be Willing to Work Long Hours

As I have alluded to throughout this book, sales, especially in the early years, requires long hours and lots of effort if you want to succeed. Shortcuts to success in this field don't exist. If you can't manage the long, demanding hours, then your success will not be assured. If, on the other hand, you can outwork your competitors and peers, there is no limit to what you will be able to accomplish over time.

How to Prepare for Long Hours

Long hours and endless days require a lot of energy, without any immediate positive return. But you can do some things to make sure you have the time, energy, and attitude to put in long hours on the job. Figure out what works for you.

Recipes for Success

You know that you have to study, put in your time, and have a positive attitude to succeed. But how do you do all that without burning out? Each person is different, but the following is a list of some essentials for optimum performance in your life:

- Eat a balanced diet.
- Manage the stressors in your life.
- Eliminate destructive mental and physical habits that will sabotage your energy.
- Play hard.
- Get regular exercise.
- Take mini vacations.
- If you need to lose weight, do it.
- Nap on weekends when you can.
- Get to bed an hour earlier every night.
- Take vitamin supplements.

There are other actions that will help, but this list will get you started, and if you can do many of them, you will be amazed at how much energy you will have for the demanding tasks ahead.

How to Manage Working Long Hours

Many of the methods or ideas I suggested in the previous section take time, commitment, discipline, and persistence. There is no easy way to accomplish what you want. To do so you will need to manage your time better, and arrange your priorities and resources in your life and career with care.

Sacrifice

Unquestionably, to be successful, you must be willing to sacrifice many of your personal needs and agendas. It is important to have personal goals as well as career and sales goals. We have already discussed this topic in a previous chapter. In this section I would like to offer a little different perspective. Often your personal and career or business goals may conflict with each other. Welcome to the real world. You can't avoid this, unless you happen to consider human relationships as important as your job. If you do not have clear goals in all areas of your life, you may tend to make sacrifices in either personal or career objectives for the wrong reasons. The secret to ensuring the least amount of disruption in any area of your life due to the demands of your career is to know *why* you are doing what you are doing. Many people who set goals fail to ask themselves the critical question: Why do I want this? When you have answered this question, you will have a clearer understanding as to your real motives and how you can minimize the negative impact that these motives will have on your personal life or family circumstances.

Often your personal and career or business goals may come in conflict with each other. Welcome to the real world. There is no way to avoid this circumstance.

Preparing to Sacrifice

You must consider other factors here, not the least of which are your personal opinions, expectations, and philosophy. Often some of these might conflict with your management team or organizational philosophy. For example, let's say that your religion prohibits you from working on Sunday. What if you have a sales meeting or have to travel to a trade show on a Sunday? How will you handle this conflict? Some organizations and managers will be relatively sensitive to your personal beliefs while others won't give a rip about your family, personal interests, or religious beliefs. I am not saying this is right or wrong—it's just the way it is in the world in which you have chosen to work.

The point is, sooner or later, you may have to decide how you are going to handle the conflict between your professional expectations

Sleeping on the Job

I recall that in my early career, I was tired a lot. I can also remember losing business because my competitors got to my prospects before I did. One in particular comes to mind.

I was in my first year of sales, and I had a tremendous opportunity to close one of the biggest sales in the history of the company. It required lots of planning, preparation, and research that I had to do evenings and on a few consecutive weekends. At the time I had my priorities wrong and put off some of the work because I was just too tired and needed a break from the pressure and sheer workload. Needless to say, I lost the sale to a competitor who was better prepared and able to stick with the workload until he was done. I will never forget that early lesson. And, trust me, it will never happen again. I may lose the business because I don't have the wisdom, experience, knowledge, support, and tools, but I will never lose another sale because I am not energetic enough to be up to the task.

and your personal needs. Recognize that there may be little that you can do other than attempt to persuade your manager that your personal desires or obligations are important to you and that you respectfully request that he or she honor them. Sometimes they will; often they will not. If you chose to remain with a company or manager in which work always comes first, you must accept the consequences. Alternatively, you may look for a sales job that will be satisfying professionally but also has managers who are more aware of and sensitive to employees' personal lives.

Managing Conflict and Achieving Balance

What, then, can you do if a conflict arises between your career and some aspect of your personal life?

First, reevaluate how important this attitude, philosophy, need, or desire really is to you. Second, if it is a family issue, discuss it with your spouse to see if he or she is willing to be flexible or give at all on the issue. Third, discuss it with your manager to see if you can find an alternative solution that will work for everyone. Fourth, be open and willing to develop a new paradigm. Fifth, if necessary, be willing to stand your ground, recognizing that you may win the battle but lose the war. In other words, think about whether the short-term gain outweighs any long-term loss.

Life is often about the ability to manage change and uncertainty in a positive way; to see new situations, challenges, and circumstances from a different perspective, and to be willing to let go of expectations, habits, rules, and opinions that may have served you well in the past but are no longer in your best interests.

> *Life is often about the ability to manage change and uncertainty in a positive way.*

Prevention

One way to reduce the stress and negative outcomes of these issues is to discuss many of them with your supervisor early in your career.

I remember, years ago, when I was in sales, and my spouse gave birth to our first child. Although I loved her dearly, she never slept more than three or four hours a day. My wife at the time was exhausted and needed me to help a lot more with our daughter's care. My boss's attitude was that you can't be representing our company and selling successfully if you are also babysitting. My response was that if I had to deal with the added stress of an exhausted mother of a daughter of whom I was equally a parent, I wouldn't be very effective as a salesperson either. We reached a compromise. I adjusted my schedule so that I could satisfy his needs as well as my own needs, and those of my wife and daughter. It wasn't easy, but it did allow me to keep my job and succeed. I would make prospecting calls and do all of the studying I needed to at home. My boss made an exception in my case because I was working to do my part as well. I didn't expect a one-way solution.

The Juggling Act

Essential as well is the ability to handle multiple and various tasks simultaneously.

At any given time, you may be required to: solve after-sales problems with several customers at once; negotiate with in-house support staff for schedules, resources, or allocation of funds; prospect for new business; attend meetings; conduct research for a new customer or prospect; learn a new product for your customers; attend classes or seminars on sales skills or product applications; or do a variety of reports on territory status, customer potential, market conditions, or competitor strengths and weaknesses. This is just the beginning, and you will have to do all of this simultaneously. It may seem like a great deal to have on your plate, but remember, the more successful you become the more you will have to juggle at once.

Think About It

◆ ◆ ◆

The type of the obstacles you overcome will have a direct relationship to your success and personal satisfaction.

You might reasonably conclude, then, why become more successful if the result will be more work? This is the attitude that many salespeople take, and it leads to their ultimate failure. The longer you are in your position, the easier it will be to handle all of the additional responsibilities. With time, you will, I hope, develop strategies, habits, and approaches that enable you to pour it on without having to work that much harder. The key is to learn to work more effectively or smarter, not harder. This is a skill that you can only gain with time. You have to learn the ropes—what you can do and what you can't, on whom you can count and who is not as reliable, what resources you have at your disposal and which ones you lack.

The key is to learn the lessons as you go along and as they are presented to you. Resist the tendency to put off learning anything you can in this regard. A little extra effort in the beginning will pay handsome dividends later in your career.

The longer you are in your position, the easier it will be to handle all of the additional responsibilities.

How to Multitask

In the section on time and territory management, I shared a number of strategies to help you in this area. If you feel you are weak in this regard, you might want to go back and re-read that section. You will find many ideas on how to manage your time and responsibilities effectively.

Here are a few others to think about:

- Always spend the time necessary to do a task right the first time.
- Be careful that you don't get into a rut thinking that these responsibilities are unimportant. They are the reason you are working, and if you do them correctly, they will be the source of your success.
- Do one thing at a time.
- Learn to focus and concentrate and avoid distractions.
- Recognize that some things will always be more important than others; keep things in perspective.
- Avoid doing the easy things first, or the things you can get done quickly. You may get more done, but are you getting the right things done?
- Keep asking yourself, is this the best use of my time *now?*
- Once a day/week/month, reevaluate your priorities.
- Spend adequate time planning your day/week/month/year.

The absolute key to multitasking? That's simple: plan, plan, and plan some more.

Staying Motivated

Motivation is an inside-out proposition. Yes, some people are motivated by money, rewards, and threats, but in the long run, these are temporary. The keys to maintaining your personal motivation in good times, as well as bad, are to understand the essence of motivation and how it affects you personally.

What Motivates You?

Everyone is motivated. Not everyone, though, is motivated by the same things. Some people get a rush when they are given a plaque in front of 100 people, while others only need the quiet satisfaction of knowing they have overcome an obstacle and accomplished a goal. Some people measure their success and ability to stay motivated by how much money they make.

The key to effective personal motivation is to keep in the forefront of your consciousness those things (reasons) for which you are doing what you are doing.

I am not saying that any of these are better or worse than any others or that some are right and others wrong. The key to effective motivation is to know what motivates you and why. If you have never taken stock of this issue, now is the time to do it. It is also important to know what makes you unmotivated. Often eliminating something that strips your motivation is just as valuable as having a positive motivator.

The key to effective personal motivation is to keep in the forefront of your consciousness those things (reasons) for which you are doing what you are doing. It is also important to recognize that the more control you have over your motivators, the more likely you are to remain motivated, regardless of the circumstances. For example, if you are motivated by money and your company changes the sales compensation plan in midstream (yes, it happens all the time), you may find yourself losing your motivation, and there is nothing you can do to change the circumstances.

If, in contrast, you are motivated by completing a task, and you can control the circumstances surrounding its completion, guess what—you can better control the events that determine your personal motivation. Don't get me wrong; there is nothing inherently bad in any form of positive motivation. Sales contests can be good for you and your motivation, but they can also reduce motivation for others.

The point is to be sure that you have some control over whatever motivates you. Even a redesigned sales compensation program can give you the opportunity to reevaluate how you are selling and to whom, to see if you can't improve your performance and income in spite of the new program.

Be sure to have some control over what motivates you.

In this chapter I have tried to illuminate the realities in the sales profession. If you feel I am being negative, or you are wondering what you got yourself into, you may want to read more about the profession—or change careers. Reality does not disappear because we choose not to see it. It is better to be prepared than be broadsided by circumstances, events, or people—something that you could have avoided if you had had ample warning and heeded those warnings.

Let me repeat, I have made my living for over forty years selling. I love it. I love the freedom, independence, success, ability to help others and yes, the money. But I also love the challenges, problems, risks, and even the failures. It is all part of the game. Remember, you will win some, and you will lose some. You won't win them all nor will you lose them all. I can tell you, though, the smell and taste of victory far outweigh the negative experiences of defeat and failure.

Good Stuff

During your first year, you will have many successes as you learn new skills and contribute to the lives of your customers. Your primary responsibility in sales is to help your customers improve their businesses and/or personal success, eliminate challenges and problems, and generally help them improve the quality of their lives, no matter what you sell. Many salespeople believe their major role is to improve the success of the organization that they themselves work for while earning an income. Yes, these activities are important to your overall long-term success, but you can accomplish them in many ways. It is unfortunate that some of these salespeople shade the truth, mislead customers, and often even lie to make a sale. Your personal satisfaction and self-esteem can only come from an ethical approach to your position and its responsibilities.

On Success (and Frustration)

In the course of your career, if you choose to follow the high moral ground, you will undoubtedly experience many situations in which you can be proud of your accomplishments. When you create win-win relationships with your customers or clients you will set yourself up for an unlimited amount of positive feedback, accolades, genuine appreciation, and often written and oral thanks that will compensate for all of the negatives you may also experience. Selling is a worthy career. It gives you the opportunity to make a difference in your customers' and clients' lives, and when you do, you can go to sleep at night knowing full well that you have made a wise choice in selecting this career.

Your personal satisfaction and self-esteem can only come from an ethical approach to your position and its responsibilities.

Real Success

During my sales career I have received over three thousand letters of thanks for a job well done. I have included a couple of them in this chapter. Let me tell you, when I have seriously felt that the difficulties of this profession were so overwhelming that I wanted to quit and get a "regular" job, it was these letters that kept me going.

Now, when you are in a slump, down in the dumps, the world has turned its back on you, your manager is breathing down your neck, you haven't made a sale in three months, and you just can't take another day, you will feel a renewed sense of purpose after receiving a genuine and heartfelt thanks from one of your customers or clients. The key is to perform in such a way that people offer such accolades truthfully and frequently.

Thank Me Now and Thank Me Later

What are some things that you can do to deserve letters and appreciation like this from customers, clients, fellow salespeople, support staff, or even your suppliers?

Go the extra mile. Doing more for your customers than they ask, deserve, or even pay for. It means you are more concerned with what they get than how you benefit from a sale to them. Promise a lot and deliver more. Most salespeople promise a little and deliver less.

Give rather than receive. Develop the philosophy of giving rather than getting. This means that in the normal routines of your daily tasks you take

Real Success—Part One

Years ago, I gave each employee of one of my clients a copy of a book I wrote. Several weeks later I received a letter from one of the employees:

"Tim, the words in your book came at a time when I was facing a serious crossroads in my career. I was discouraged, frustrated, unhappy, and ready to throw in the towel. After reading your words, I felt a renewed sense of dedication and commitment. I decided to give it all I could and never consider failure as an option. At the time the future was as bleak as it could be for anyone, anywhere. I was failing due to a loss of belief, passion, confidence, and dedication. I was looking more for how I would benefit than how my customers would from my relationship with them. Your words gave me a new perspective. Today, years later, I am one of my company's most successful and respected executives. I can only imagine what my life would have been like today had I not developed a new attitude. Thank you for saving my life and career."

That is why you do your job, everyday.

the time to think about others more than yourself. It requires a loss of selfishness on your part. This will take adjusting of your own self-expectations, and for some this is not an easy task.

Real Success—Part Two

After conducting an in-house, three-day custom management seminar I received the following e-mail.

"Tim, our business was on the brink of failure. Our customers were bailing out faster than they were coming in, our employees were leaving in droves, and my personal life was in shambles as a result. Your program couldn't have come at a better time. As a result of the information you shared, we are back on track headed for a record-breaking year. New customers are lining up to do business with us, we are turning away potential new employees because we just don't have the physical space for them, and my relationship with my spouse and children couldn't be better. I can't thank you enough for your insight, wisdom, ability to challenge us in a positive way, and your concern for our success."

Deliver More Value. Develop the habit of spending some time every day to do a little extra for some of your customers without expecting a thank you or a response. Do it because it is who you are, not because of what you will receive in return. You can send them an article you thought they might enjoy or benefit from that doesn't have anything to do with improving their business or your products or services. You do it because you want to send the message—I care about you, not just your business.

Focus and learn. Learn to focus on what you are learning and how it will help others, not only you or your organization. Spend time learning about your customers' industries, concerns, needs, and expectations that have nothing to do with your product or service. Get inside their business. I remember years ago having dinner with several employees of one of my clients. One of the sales managers said over coffee, "You have been doing business with our company for over five years, and we no longer think of you as an outsider, but one of us. As a result, we know that your only interest is our success and not your own." That statement made my month!

Appreciate. Show appreciation for the things that people do for you. People in general tend to want to do more for those who show appreciation about what is done for them. Whether it is a thank-you call, letter, or note doesn't matter. Just that you have taken the time to notice and acknowledge their thoughtfulness will go a long way in building favorable

long-term relationships. I'll prove it. Who do you tend to want to do more for? People who say thank you or people who act like they deserve it or you owe it to them?

Show that you care. Show people you care and are thinking about them or are interested in them by sending them birthday cards, flowers, or special recognition of some kind. I give away over two thousand books a year to people just to say thanks. I send out over fifty greeting cards a month acknowledging special events like business anniversaries, new product introductions, promotions, and numerous other special events. You would be amazed at how few salespeople go to the trouble or expense to take these kinds of actions. Trust me, sooner or later it will pay off, not necessarily financially (but it can there as well), but in many other ways, that during the course of your career will give you far more positive and lasting satisfaction and meaning than your last paycheck or award.

Acknowledge your staff. Get in the habit of thanking and praising support staff for their effort on your behalf. Yes, they are paid to do the work, but a little praise and appreciation can go along way. I remember in my first sales position, there was one secretary for the entire sales staff. Now, I ask you, if you need a proposal done on the computer or are out of town and need some samples sent to a prospect and there are ten other salespeople vying for this person's

Think About It

• • •

Don't wait for others to give you what you can give yourself—pat yourself on the back when you feel you deserve it.

time, which salesperson's request is going to get handled first if he or she can't get to everything today? You guessed it—the one who was requested by the person who is the most appreciative and thankful. I learned this lesson the hard way. I lost a sale because my proposal wasn't on the top of the pile one day. The tasks that got her attention were the ones not necessarily requested by the most successful or longest-term salesperson on the staff, but for the ones who were the most respectful, kind, appreciative, and courteous.

Say thank you. Don't underestimate the power of thanking your manager for his or her help and support. Your manager has a great deal to handle. You are not the only one who wants and needs direction, support, guidance, and praise. Your manager has responsibilities up the chain of command as well as down. He or she also has a manager who has to be kept informed and met with. Managers have reports, business obligations, and most likely family obligations as well. Your manager is going to do his or her best to spread time, talent, and resources around as well as possible. Accept that you are not their only responsibility. Showing them routinely that you appreciate their time and effort on your behalf will go a long way in ensuring that you get their time and support when you need or want it most.

Remember other departments. If it is appropriate in your position—and this can depend on what you sell—every once in a while show gratitude to the people in finance, distribution, manufacturing, design, customer service, human resources, and administration.

These people are all on your team, and you need to have people willing to go to bat for you in a crunch.

Remember everyone. Show appreciation for the efforts of your vendors or suppliers on your behalf. Your suppliers have other responsibilities than to help you succeed. They have other customers as well. Whether it is requesting them to join you on a sales call, to tracking down an order or just following up with a customer, you will want them to be available for you when you need them. The only way to ensure this support is to let them know how much you appreciate their concern and help.

Acknowledge experience. Be thankful to the more veteran salespeople on your staff for their help and guidance. Sooner or later you will need to ask for the help of one of the more senior members of your sales team. They, too, have their own customers' demands and their career issues. In fact, because they have been employed there longer, I'll bet they have a lot more on their plate than you do. Appreciate their guidance and support. It could prove invaluable in saving you time, mistakes, and even failure over time.

Thank your spouse. And finally, show appreciation and understanding to your spouse if you have one, for his or her patience while you devote a great deal of your energy and time to your career. It is critical that you maintain a healthy personal life while you are in your new career. At times, you may need to miss a meal, weekend, special event, or simply a night at home with your family. But keep this to a minimum, for ultimately it will impact your career. A personal life that is in shambles will eventually play havoc with your career and its success. Regularly show your appreciation to those in your life that really matter. Tell them you understand the sacrifices they are making so you can have a successful career.

> *A personal life that is in shambles will eventually play havoc with your career and its success.*

The previous list might leave you thinking that all you will have time for is to go around thanking people every day and that you won't have any time left to sell. This attitude of thankfulness is more a function of who you are than how you spend your time. Really, how long or how much effort does it take to give a support person a few words of praise once or twice a week?

Handling Recognition (or Lack Thereof)

As wonderful and necessary as recognition is, if you don't handle it properly or you don't get enough you will have to deal with this in a professional manner. Following are a few problems with recognition that you may experience, particularly early in your career.

No thank you's. What if you feel like you are not getting enough recognition? As a new salesperson, you will want to know how you are doing as you progress in your new career position. If your expectation is to have every deed recognized, you will set yourself up for a great deal of frustration. Your manager, depending on his/her competence, available time, and the size of his or her sales team may not give you the feedback you want or need during your first months. Learn to accept the reality that your value is not directly related to who notices what you do, or how well or how often you do it.

Unequal recognition. Someone else on the sales team gets more recognition than you do for the same results, activities, or success. In your early career, your major concern should be how well you are doing, not keeping track of others. This is not a race or a competition with the other members of the sales staff. This is about your success and your personal pace. As long as you are learning and doing your best with what you are learning and doing, forget everyone else and what they get and how often. Believe me, if you focus on your own growth and not the psychological need for a pat on the back every morning, you will survive and prosper. However, if your major concern is recognition, sooner or later I guarantee you will be disappointed and frustrated. Both of these emotions can take your eye off the ball.

A swelled head. You receive recognition and it goes to your head. I have seen this happen more often than you can imagine. I have seen people fail in their sales position after getting salesperson of the month or year.

> ## Punch Your Own Ticket
>
>
> Years ago I heard a speaker give the following example. I think it bears repeating here. She said, "Many people go through life holding out a ticket to be punched over time if they do something well." Many organizations use a similar approach. Go into a coffee shop and when you buy a latte, they punch your ticket. Get ten punches and you receive a free latte. She went on to say, "The secret to happiness and emotional well-being is to learn to punch your own ticket when you do something good. Don't wait or expect others to notice, care, or bother to punch your ticket." I thought this was great advice and have used it ever since. Later in this chapter I'll show you how I have adapted it to suit my personal needs.

Strange? Yes. True? Yes. Why? I could give you numerous examples from the field of business, sports, entertainment, and education. Let's use sports as an illustration. How many teams have repeated back-to-back championships in football, baseball or basketball? How many people have won consecutive tournaments in tennis? Golf? Oh yes, there are some examples, but fewer rather than more. Why? Is it arrogance? Overconfidence? They stop learning or growing? They lose their passion, drive, focus or commitment? You tell me! To avoid this trap, learn that any recognition you receive, although nice and even earned, it is not why you will succeed. You will succeed because of your effort, commitment, willingness to learn, and many of the topics we have discussed in this book up to this point.

Think About It

◆ ◆ ◆

Rewards are not always financial. The feeling of a "job well done" or that you helped someone can be worth a great deal.

No praise. You only get negative feedback and you never get any praise. Some managers are uncomfortable giving positive praise or feedback. Many are only capable of negative reinforcement. If you are unfortunate enough to be working for someone like that there are some steps you can take:

- Keep a journal of your successes and positive deeds.
- Start a good stuff jar.
- Spend time with your mentor.
- Meet with your manager and discuss why the only feedback you receive is negative (make sure you are on solid ground here and really deserve it).
- Ask your manager what you have to do to earn his or her praise or positive feedback.
- Ask your fellow sales team members for positive feedback.
- Rely on the positive feedback and praise from your customers as enough.

There are numerous other recognition issues, but most that you will face will tend to fall into the above five categories. The key thing to remember is that the only recognition that really matters is that which you receive from your customers. Remember, that's why your company is in business, and it is the major responsibility of your career to always ensure that the customer comes first. Some companies do not have this philosophy. Just remember, no matter what your organization's philosophy is, without customers, none of you has a job. So, the only recognition that matters comes from your satisfied customers. Work for it, and you will never have to worry about how successful you will be or whether you have a job tomorrow.

Setting and Reaching Higher Goals

In an earlier chapter we discussed in detail the importance of setting goals and how to move towards them. My intent here is not to repeat the earlier discussion, but to take it to a higher level.

Once you understand the goal-setting process and its importance, you will realize that your continued success is directly related to your ability to set bigger and more challenging objectives and goals. Your early goals might have been to:

- Improve your product knowledge.
- Master the fundamental sales skills.
- Learn new attitudes that would guarantee your survival.
- Reach your quota.
- Fill your prospect pipeline.
- Satisfy the expectations of your manager.
- Make a living.
- Increase your income.

Now it is time to move beyond the basics and begin to think longer term and broader. It is time to accept the fact that you have survived, you are doing well, you like the role of selling and what it gives you, and you need bigger and more challenging

Think About It

• • •

Ask for testimonial letters from your clients and keep them in a binder. Whenever you feel discouraged, read them.

goals in order to continue to grow in your career. From personal experience, I have learned that:

- Increased recognition doesn't do it.
- More money doesn't do it.
- More freedom doesn't do it.
- Greater leverage doesn't do it.
- More knowledge doesn't do it.
- Being number one doesn't do it.

Then what does? That, my friend, is what you have to determine for yourself. I can only give you a few guidelines to consider. Here is what you will have to learn as you begin to reach for more in your career and life:

1. What keeps the passion growing for you in your career and life?
2. If you didn't have to work, how would you spend your time?
3. When do you feel really good about yourself?
4. Why do you want to earn more money?
5. If your manager said, "You will no longer be paid for your effort and results" would you continue in this career? Would you work for free? I know, I know, seems like a foolish question. But consider you no longer need the money. You are secure due to your wise management and investment of your income over the years.
6. Do you like the intangible benefits of this career, the ability to help others enough to stick with it for different motives?
7. Do you love the problems and challenges as much as the results and success?
8. Do you enjoy helping others or are you in it for yourself?

9. Do you want to move into management and beyond?
10. Would you like to start your own business someday?
11. Is retirement an option for you? Or do you love what you do so much you never want to stop or do something else?

That's enough to get you started. Why not spend some time on these questions and then come up with some additional ones of your own? Make them challenging and thought-provoking. The value of the answers in life is related to the quality of the questions.

Taking the Good Stuff and Leaving the Bad Stuff Behind

One of the skills necessary for success in sales is the ability to compartmentalize, to keep the good stuff in your consciousness and the negative stuff quarantined like a computer virus. What is bad stuff? I am confident everyone will define this differently. To me, the bad stuff are those circumstances or events that: a) negatively impact your attitudes b) take your eyes off what is really important c) prevent your personal or career growth d) cause you to fail. Bad is *not*: problems, but the inability to learn from them; failures, but your inability to overcome them; setbacks, but your unwillingness to find another way. Bad stuff can be good stuff. And, good stuff can potentially be bad stuff. Good, bad, bad, good; so what? As you can see, it really only matters what you do with it not what it is.

Bad is not: problems, but rather the inability to learn from them; failures, but rather your inability to overcome them; setbacks, but rather your unwillingness to find another way.

Everyone, sooner or later, does something they feel is worthy of praise or recognition. One of the things I learned early in my career was that if I didn't blow my own horn, nobody would ever know how

Good Versus Bad

So what are some of the bad things that could impact your career success and what are some of the good things that can help you build on your success? The bad stuff:

- Making a sale too early in your career and coming to the conclusion that this is really easy. Thinking "I don't have to learn the skills or develop the attitudes. Man, this career is a snap."
- Doing anything negative or misleading (even lying) to make a sale.
- Refusing to grow and learn.
- Arrogance; thinking you are better than others because you may be selling more. You may be more successful, but that doesn't make you better than anyone.

good I was or what I had done that I felt deserved recognition. I remember one time after several years in sales I was not getting the recognition I believed I deserved from a client for helping them solve a serious problem. When I asked the client why he hadn't thanked me, he gave me the classic answer that has stayed with me for years. "That's your job, to help me solve my problems. Why do I need to thank you?" My first reaction was to say, "Yes, that's true but a simple thank you would be nice." I didn't say it, but I learned a valuable lesson. If you want to get any recognition, sooner or later you are going to have to learn to blow your own horn or self-promote. The most successful people I know today are great at self-promotion. I won't mention any personal names, but how about Cassius Clay (Mohammed Ali), whose most famous remark was, "I am the greatest." He said that before he was. How about the last year of politicians in the United States? Most—right or wrong, good or bad—are great self-promoters.

There's more, but I don't want you to think I am too negative. How about the good stuff:

- Helping a customer solve a problem.
- Contributing to the success of your company.
- Offering support and growth to a fellow salesperson so he or she can make a sale.
- Getting recognized for a major accomplishment.
- Winning a sales contest.
- Exceeding your quota.
- Making more money than you thought possible.

Again, there are lots more of the positives as well. See how many you can think of.

Keeping a Personal Success Journal

What is a personal success journal? It is not a diary. It is a tool to help you achieve greater success and remember what you have achieved in your career and life. Your journal can be as simple as a three ring binder notebook or a fancy perfect bound journal that you purchase in a giftshop or bookstore. The point is it doesn't matter what you use as long as you:

- Get in the habit of writing in it every day.
- Record your successes and achievements no matter how small or trivial they might seem.
- Use it to keep track of your progress reaching your goals.
- Keep it positive and upbeat.
- Don't editorialize as you write (you can be the only one who ever reads it).

- Don't leave anything out.
- Start today.

I have been keeping a journal for more than twenty years. My only mistake was not starting earlier in my career. It is so easy to forget all of the things we have learned, shared, and accomplished in our lives if we don't have a system for recording them. Here are a few things I keep in my journal:

- Lessons learned.
- Insights I have experienced.
- Goals I have set.
- Goals I have accomplished.
- Special recognitions I have earned.
- Special quotes I have run across.
- Books I have read.
- Books I want to read.
- Places I have visited.
- Places I want to visit.
- New skills I have developed.
- New people I have met.
- People who have helped me and how.
- Career milestones.
- Special events in my life.

I am sure you get the picture—anything that makes you feel good about yourself and your past goes in the journal.

Why keep a journal anyway? Why go to all of the trouble? That was what I thought years

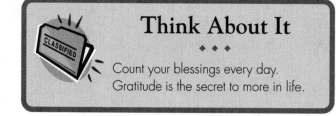

Think About It

◆ ◆ ◆

Count your blessings every day.
Gratitude is the secret to more in life.

ago and didn't take early advice from a mentor that I keep a journal. Well, I can only tell you that a great deal of the material in my journal has helped me through more than one setback or failure and times of discouragement in my life. When life gets difficult, and you are not sure if it (whatever) is worth the continued effort, struggle, or commitment, referring back to your journal will give you the confidence and patience to persevere. My journal reminds me of how far I have come and how good I am, not compared to anyone else, but compared to how good I was five, ten, even twenty years ago. Don't wait: Start your personal success journal today.

Creating a Good Stuff Wall and Jar

I know what you are thinking. A good stuff jar? What's that, anyway? Several years ago I started a good stuff jar and a good stuff wall.

Good stuff jar. It is just what it sounds like—a large jar that I purchased at a department store that sits on my desk. Any time I accomplish anything worthwhile or want to put something in the jar that reminds me of some special time in my life or event—I write it down and put it in the jar. Today as I write I can see it on my desk, crammed full of stuff. What's in my jar? Well, a:

- Copy of the check I received as an advance from the publisher for this book.
- Testimonial letter I received from a special client.
- Wonderful birthday card I received from my son on my fifty-eighth birthday.
- Note from a friend thanking me for a special consideration.
- Copy of a check for the biggest sale I have made in my speaking career.
- Picture my granddaughter made for me when she was visiting last summer.

- Photo I took while on vacation to Spain.
- Copy of an e-mail I received from a customer who purchased one of my books
- Copy of a royalty check from the publisher of my first book, *Soft Sell.*

Remember: To know and not do is to not know.

What's the value of a good stuff jar? Well, it is very similar to my success journal. Whenever I feel a little discouraged, down, or as if I might like to quit, (yes, even authors have their bad days) I just reach in the jar and pull out a handful, and look at, read, or reflect on the contents. You would be amazed at what this can do to melt away your frustration, anxiety, or sense of loss or discouragement. Try it for a few months. Put anything and everything in it that has special meaning for you, and I will bet before you know it, you will need a second jar.

Take some time to reflect on what you read in this chapter as well as what you are going to do with it. Remember: To know and not do is to not know.

Traits of Sales Superstars

No matter how good you are, you can always reach a higher level. Often, each "next step" takes a little more effort to ascend than the previous one did. But read on: The more you know about what it takes to continue your rise to stardom, the easier it will be to reach the top.

Going to the Next Level

I have observed thousands of salespeople during my years of sales training. I have found that there are twenty-four ways in which these pros take quantum leaps ahead of their competition. Want to move to the next higher level in sales? Then adopt the principles that appear on the following pages as your guiding philosophy.

Sales leaders have passion. They are more passionate about their opportunity to be of service, to learn, to improve their status and their lifestyles. They are more passionate about their organizations' products and services. They are passionate about developing their sales and human–relationship skills. Sales leaders are more passionate about life. They see life as an adventure, not as the "same stuff, different day." If you want to be a sales leader, you must be passionate about your job and your future.

In addition, they are passionate about solving their clients' problems. And they are passionate about learning everything they can about their customers' business. For them, passion comes from within; it is not something they try to impose on themselves or have to force. There is a fire inside them, and it is reflected in their eyes. Do you have the passion to make your clients' and customers' wants and needs priority one?

Sales leaders go the extra mile. In an age when organizations are handing their salespeople a great deal to do—sell, market, service, administer, promote, solve problems, and so on—it is no wonder that poor salespeople have less time to sell and learn. Successful salespeople promise a lot and deliver even more than they promise. But to accomplish this, they must manage their time, activities, and resources with precision. Going the extra mile means doing more for a customer than the customer expects them to do, demands, or pays for. It is doing all the little extras that communicates that they care and that their clients' business is important to them. This philosophy helps them build solid relationships that are not impervious to

Think About It

◆ ◆ ◆

It is what you do *today* that will make you a star in the future.

competition, but are certainly unskilled salespeople selling lower prices and empty promises.

Sales leaders are a resource. Poor salespeople sell products, services, features, benefits, what's available, the solutions to problems, price, and any number of other specific or general commodities. The pros who put distance between themselves and their nearest competitors sell themselves as resources for their clients. As resources, sales leaders are asked for their advice, counsel, and opinions on many related or unrelated issues. They regularly bring creative ideas and information to their customers. Their clients look forward to their visits and telephone calls because they know they will bring value to them rather than arriving with no more than the desire to sell another service or new product.

Sales leaders are more passionate about life. They see life as an adventure, not as the "same stuff, different day."

Sales leaders are creative. Every day, you could find thousands of people who would tell you that there's nothing new under the sun. They're wrong. These people are living either in fantasyland or on some island that's removed from civilization. Every day, thousands of new inventions, new kinds of technology, new approaches—whatever you can think of, are being invented or improved. Salespeople who keep the business once they get it know that they must also keep the vigil for new, creative ideas, solutions, and information that can help their customers compete better and succeed more. To keep up with the tremendous flow of new ideas, they constantly seek out information and publications, like this one, that keep them abreast of changes that might affect their current or future clients.

Sales leaders invest in themselves. The key to success in the coming years is personal growth. The pros that are outdistancing their nearest competitors are doing so because they have better skills, greater understanding, and increased awareness—and they integrate this information into their daily sales activity. Personal growth means many different things to different people. What I am referring to here is the consistent pursuit of knowledge that will allow them to continue to compete and win in the marketplace of tomorrow. It takes time, money, and commitment to devote yourself to a path of self-improvement. But these pros know that the payoff will far exceed the cost.

Sales leaders are authentic and real. Vulnerability and humility are valuable traits. People who act their way through life must expend a great deal of energy, constantly, in maintaining their facades. People who behave as they really are, in contrast, can focus on being. The pros are consistent in their behavior because that behavior comes from a constant set of core values, beliefs, and attitudes. They are comfortable with who they are and are not looking for approval or acceptance of their behavior. In the truest sense, they are real. When you meet them, you can see this in their actions and decisions. They live with an inner integrity. They are not trying to be anything or anyone else, and they are inner-directed, not outer-directed.

Think About It

♦ ♦ ♦

What defines real superstars is not what they take from life but rather what they give in life.

Sales leaders love what they are doing. People who live with inner acceptance, peace, and harmony also live spontaneously. Successful and happy people spend their time in the present. With this philosophy, they enjoy and live life to the fullest. In other words, they have fun. They are fun to be with. They don't take life or themselves too seriously. They know that business is only a game. They win some and lose some, but they know that when they lose, they can also grow, and that when they win, they also gain new opportunities. Their definition of winning is beating their own personal best, not beating other people.

Sales leaders focus on service. Ineffective salespeople focus on what they get, while the pros focus on what the customer gets. Their sole purpose is to serve. And they know that in this service, they build reputations and lifestyles that testify to this philosophy. They believe that if the client ever loses or perceives that they have lost, they, the salespeople, loses as well. To these salespeople, service is the foundation that underlies everything they do. Sales leaders' financial success rests on being there *first*, being there *last*, and being there *when they are needed*.

Sales leaders cultivate support. Successful salespeople know that they can't always get the answers their customers need or solve their clients' problems without the support of other people, both inside and outside their organization. They are the customers' ambassador inside their organizations. Sales leaders build bridges of support with customer service reps, executives, and anyone else they need to help serve their customer in a satisfactory way. They are firm and unyielding, yet friendly and compassionate when dealing with other people. They build bridges of understanding and cooperation.

Sales leaders build bridges of support with customer service reps, executives, and anyone else they need to help serve their customer in a satisfactory way.

Sales leaders go to bed late and get up early. They work hard. They know that their customers' needs, desires, and problems are the central reason that they are in that relationship. They have heard about working smart, but they know it is not a substitute for effort. They don't even consider what they do as work. They don't follow the clock or the calendar. They love the holidays, all 365 of them. They love it all, even the parts they don't really like. They have learned to love to do the things they don't like to do.

Sales leaders believe. They believe in themselves, their mission, their organization, their products and services, their management, and the free marketplace that permits them to help others while they help themselves. Their self-belief is a fiber that is woven into everything they do. They have high expectations of themselves, their organization's ability to perform, and their clients' willingness to give them business. They build strong relationships that, even though they may be tested from time to time, can withstand the miscommunication and errors that will inevitably occur.

Sales leaders are focused. They know that it is critical to maintain focus. Every day, every activity, every sales call, and every working moment, they are aiming at a specific target. They believe that to be effective, they must do one thing at a time. They will have multiple projects going on simultaneously, but moment by moment, they are only working on one. They know the tremendous power of singleness of purpose.

Sales leaders break the rules. Effective salespeople don't follow conventional wisdom. They have learned that conventional wisdom is more often wrong than right. Sales leaders push the edges in all areas of their life. They are never satisfied with the status quo. Their motto is: It can be better. I can be better. I can do it better.

Sales leaders push the edges in all areas of their life. They are never satisfied with the status quo.

Sales leaders are here, there, and everywhere. To succeed in today's world, exposure is critical. These salespeople know that their customers are their competitors' best prospects. They network, they collect business cards, and they attend meetings and seminars looking for new contacts who will contribute to their careers. They appear to be everywhere. They don't waste their time, but they target their exposure. They ensure that each exposure keeps them on the right track. They are not looking to simply add names to their database but to collect relationships that can aid their careers.

Sales leaders are macro thinkers. They see the big picture. They know that they must handle the details, but their creative thought patterns focus on the macro issues. They don't get bogged down in petty, negative, or small thinking. They pay attention to the terrain immediately in front of them while at the same time seeing the mountain on the horizon. They are big dreamers. They know that they won't always reach their goals on schedule, but they always shoot further and higher than they or even the world thinks is possible. Their attitude is: why not? What have I got to lose? They focus on the ends rather than the means.

Sales leaders study their clients' business. They are walking encyclopedias of information about their customers. They know their objectives, histories, goals, problems, frustrations, expectations, style of doing business, needs, dreams, and their people. Their customers' employees perceive them as colleagues, not adversaries. They are on the lookout for methods, tools, ideas, and information that they can bring to their clients to help them improve performance, success, income, market penetration, positive growth, and longevity.

Sales leaders study their competitors. They are not surprised when they don't get business. They know the weaknesses as well as the strengths of their competition. They know their competitors' philosophies, people, attitudes, and vulnerabilities. They freely recommend another firm if they believe that to do so is in the best long-term interests of their prospect. They know that when the prospect does business with a competitor they have recommended, they may have lost a sale, but they have not lost a potential client. And they understand the difference. They are playing the long game.

Sales leaders keep in touch. Out of sight, out of mind. Successful salespeople who put distance between themselves and their less successful counterparts know the value of staying in touch with their clients. They do this in a variety of ways. They inform them regularly about new organizational policies or procedures, new products or services, success stories, and market conditions in other industries that might affect their customers. They pass along any number of bits of information that are of potential value to clients. They do this using newsletters, faxes, letters, telephone calls, meetings, and special forums. They do not waste their clients' time with such useless approaches as, "I was in the area so I thought I would drop by."

Sales leaders are detectives. The pros spend the bulk of their time getting, not giving, information. They know that client, competitor, and market information is power. They may not have an immediate use or need for all the information they get from these sources, but they know that some day, in some way, the information they get will have value. They devour newsletters, trade periodicals, audiotapes, literature, and generally anything they can get their hands on that gives them potentially valuable information.

Sales leaders cultivate references. People like to buy from people they trust. No salesperson can know everyone who can have a positive influence on the outcome of a buying decision. Pros know that they need a stable full of satisfied clients or resources who will gladly provide positive references. They cultivate these sources. They know that even though they may not be able to get more business from them, a positive endorsement can be worth its weight in gold.

Pros know that they need a stable full of satisfied clients or resources who will gladly provide positive references.

Sales leaders ask for, and get, referrals. The best source of new business is from present clients. When I say present, I mean anyone you have ever done business with. They may not be active clients because at the present time you may not be getting any business from them, but they are always present clients. It costs more energy, time, money, resources, stress, and effort to get a new client than it does to keep one. Pros work as hard to keep the business as they did to get it. Once they have a client, they keep the relationship alive and positive through service, attention, and interest. They might not get more business from these clients, but they know that a qualified, referred new prospect from a present or active client is well worth the time and energy required to keep the client. Always nurture and maintain your existing relationships and those clients will become your allies in cultivating new business.

Sales leaders use customer profiles. It is impossible to see every possible prospect. Ineffective salespeople have the philosophy, "If they will see me, I will see them." Pros know that some prospects are better prospects than others. They also know that every customer is also a prospect. The customer profile is a template. It is a system they use to determine who is the best qualified prospect they can see now.

Poor salespeople try to turn poor prospects into customers. The pros don't have time for this kind of activity. They want to spend their limited sales time only with well-qualified prospects.

Sales leaders believe in win-win negotiation. If everyone is to feel as though they have won something in a negotiation, it is vital that the salesperson understand this critical concept in negotiation. Negotiation is never a substitute for effective sales. And it will never make up for poor sales skills. In a win-win negotiation, everybody gets something they want or need. Poor salespeople sell or negotiate on price alone. The pros who are winning in the marketplace know that although price is a concern to today's buyer, it is not, in the long term, the most important issue. Poor salespeople are always on the defensive. They are reducing prices, giving away more than they need to. Pros know that when you win with a dime, you will lose by a dime.

In a win-win negotiation, everybody gets something they want or need.

Sales leaders keep accurate records. To chart a more effective course for the future, you need to know where you have been. You need to know precisely where you must modify your behavior, improve your skills, or change your approach. Pros ask themselves regularly, "What is working? What isn't working? What did I used to do that used to work that I have stopped doing?" They keep immaculate records on activity, results, errors, mistakes, successes, and anything else they need to improve. Whether they use a journal, a spreadsheet, or some type of call report doesn't matter. What matters is that they can bring their personal history into their present, therefore changing their future.

Well, there they are. The twenty-four concepts that are used by professional salespeople who are each day putting more and more distance between themselves and their closest rivals. How are you doing? Which areas should you pay some attention to if you are to continue to compete successfully in the marketplace of tomorrow?

Keeping Your Focus in a Down Sales Cycle

We discussed earlier the concept of a sales slump. The causes of these slow periods include:

1. Poor training.
2. Poor product knowledge.
3. Poor attitude management.
4. Poor sales records.
5. Poor organization reputation.
6. Poor product quality, distribution, or organization support.
7. An organization- versus customer-focused sales strategy.
8. Sales compensation that rewards results only and is not focused on activity.
9. Excessive administrative responsibilities.
10. Poor territory potential.
11. Unsupportive management.
12. Poor sales management coaching skills.
13. Organizational culture that encourages the editing of honest communication.
14. Lack of clear purpose, goals, and focus.
15. Poor organization and time and territory management.

If you are in sales, I encourage you to examine each of these areas in detail to determine where you and your organization need to improve so that you can prevent future slumps. If you are in management, I recommend that you evaluate each area for which you are responsible, including training approaches, corporate policies, procedures, philosophy, communication patterns, sales reporting, management style, compensation programs and product/service quality, distribution, and billing issues that may contribute to poor sales performance.

Preventing Sales Slumps

Of course, it is best to simply avoid sales slumps altogether, at least as much as possible. This, however, isn't entirely a matter of luck; you need to know how to avoid slumps. What can you do to prevent a sales slump, or snap out of one if you are already there? Several things, like:

1. *Conduct a careful, honest self-evaluation of your sales-process strengths and weaknesses.*

2. *Keep a log or record of your successes as well as your needs in the areas of skill and attitude development.* When you feel discouraged, you can review all your recent, as well as long-term, gains and wins. I call this a good-stuff list. You would be amazed how quickly you can reverse a negative direction by frequently reviewing all of your successes.

3. *Learn to keep detailed records of sales activity and your results.* I am not talking here about your call reports. Even the best and most sophisticated call reports I have seen do not give adequate information about the critical sales ratios and trends that determine your future.

4. *Spend a minimum of an hour a day listening to motivational audiocassettes.*

5. *Plan your year, month, week, and day in advance.*

6. *Review your progress toward your goals daily.* Look for areas in which you have made commitments but have not followed through.

7. *Be ruthlessly honest with yourself.* Don't let yourself off the hook when you have failed to do what you said you would.

8. *When you succeed, reward yourself.* It doesn't have to be a two-week vacation. It could be a new tie or pair of earrings.

9. *At the end of each day, form the habit of reviewing your day, its gains and losses.*

10. *Don't beat yourself up because you didn't reach a goal, close a sale, or succeed.* Learn that as long as you are learning and getting better, that is enough. Be patient with yourself, but be honest as well. Remember, you are either getting better or you are falling behind, but you can't be standing still.

11. *Ask a family member or associate to be your partner in accountability.* Share your successes and your failures with them. Ask them for an objective opinion of your program and progress.

12. *Don't compare yourself with other salespeople.* You are on your own path.

Improving Your Knowledge

I don't have to tell you—I am sure that you've figured it out for yourself—the world is changing every day before your very eyes. New technology, new laws, new policies, new medicines—in every area of life, you'll find something new. In sales, maintaining an edge in your product knowledge is vital for your long-term career success. I guarantee that within the past six months or year, your organization has changed something: a product, service, policy, distribution method, marketing plan, or some other aspect of business. Your clients expect

If people are going to trust you, they have to believe you and think that you know more than they do about your product or service or the competition.

you to have the latest. You can't expect to keep using the phrases: "I don't know, I'll have to find out, I'll look into it, I'm not sure," etc. If people are going to trust you (and we have pointed out the importance of trust in a successful sales relationship numerous times), they have to believe you and think that you know more than they do about your product or service or the competition. The Internet is making it more difficult to stay ahead of your customers when it comes to product knowledge. I can only advise you: Find a way to know more than they do if you don't want to eventually be embarrassed by a prospect or customer.

Here are a few things to keep up to date on:

- The latest product/service applications.
- How different clients are using (benefiting from) your products or services.
- Your competition's latest technology, features, and benefits.
- Who is getting into your business and who is leaving.
- Why a newer product is better than a previous version.

Raising the Bar Takes Time, Practice, and Effort

To raise the bar in your career requires that you eliminate any thought that there is such a thing as a natural-born salesperson, any more than there is a natural-born pilot, athlete, or physician. There has been a myth circulating for years that people who are successful in sales have some natural skills or attitudes, or particular types of personalities.

I have been teaching people to sell for over thirty years, and it is my opinion that selling is just like any other discipline or profession in that it requires learned skills, abilities, traits, and attitudes. I emphasize the word "learned." Show me an athlete who has "natural" ability, and I will show you an athlete who will tend not to practice as hard as someone who has to develop these skills and abilities.

What are these so-called natural skills and attitudes that people believe contribute to this innate ability to sell successfully?

- An outgoing personality.
- A friendly demeanor.
- The natural ability to persuade people to buy.
- An aggressive money-driven philosophy.
- A social orientation.
- A big ego.

What does it really take to be successful in sales? In part:

- The ability to adapt to others.
- The willingness to serve and help others.
- The ability control your ego.
- The desire to control your destiny.
- Effective communication skills.
- The willingness to continue to learn and grow personally and professionally.
- A customer-driven rather than a product- or company-driven sales approach.

These are not natural tendencies, none of them. People who are willing to adapt, grow, and learn accomplish their success by effort, time, commitment, and persistence. These traits can

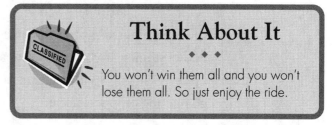

Think About It
♦ ♦ ♦
You won't win them all and you won't lose them all. So just enjoy the ride.

be in a person's genes, but people can also cultivate them over time. When they do, they incorporate them into all areas of their lives, not just sales.

So, does Michael Jordan have natural ability, or did he spend hours on the gym floor practicing? Does the figure skater Katerina Witt have natural ability, or did she spend hours on the ice practicing? All successful athletes practice for thousands of hours, developing both their inner strength and outer skills. Sales is no different. If you want to achieve excellence in sales—practice, study, implement, create, try, ask, grow, and persist.

Distinguishing Yourself

Success in an ever-changing business climate requires that you distinguish yourself and your organization from your competitors in the minds of your prospects and customers. Many products and services appear, superficially, to be identical. Printers all use ink, paper, and equipment. Staffing companies all have the same type of pool of employees, conduct similar interviews, and carry out the same testing and evaluation of potential candidates. Many computers are all the same color, have the same internal hardware, and use the same software. So how can you create, in the minds of your prospects and clients, distance between you and your products in the marketplace? You have to do it with the quality of your skills, the uniqueness of your attitudes, and the professionalism of your approach—these will increase your perceived value in the mind of the prospect and customer. If you start comparing apples to apples, you may end up representing your products as a commodity, and therefore will be competing on price alone.

There is only one way to create difference in the market with your product: by discovering the unique features or aspects of your products or services and your sales ability.

There is only one way to create difference in the market with your product: by discovering the unique features or aspects of your products or services and your sales ability. For example: Most salespeople talk too much. They

Think About It

◆ ◆ ◆

Live as if you are going to die tomorrow and work as if you are going to live forever.

launch into a feature dump, unloading information on the prospect early in the sales process. Every salesperson who sells this way is lumped into a category by the prospect as someone who is only interested in selling their product or service rather than helping the clients solve their problems or needs. On the other hand, if your approach is to ask lots of effective, pertinent, and well-timed questions before you begin to throw information on the prospect in the presentation, you will send them the message that you are different, you are a professional, and you are really interested in helping them rather than simply making the sale. To differentiate yourself, you need to establish what it is that actually makes you different, unusual, professional, or even unique from a business perspective.

I strongly recommend that you spend some time creating a list of traits, attitudes, skills, experiences, and techniques that make you truly distinctive. Once you complete the list, see if you can develop a strategy to use these differences to position yourself in the marketplace so your prospects don't think of you as being just like everyone else.

9

The Sales
Process

One of the biggest problems for many salespeople is that they do not understand that selling is a process, not an event. To sell effectively, you cannot merely close the sale, carry out better prospecting, or make more effective sales presentations—although each of these is important in its own way. Effective sales today involves blending these together in such a way that your prospects trust, believe, and respect you and your organization and want and need your product or service to help improve the quality of their lives or business enterprises.

For many years, traditional sales training focused on the "close of the sale" as the most important element. Then the 1970s and 1980s rolled around, and the hot topic was prospecting, qualifying, and getting to the key decision-makers. The 1990s brought consultative selling. What will the future bring? Who knows? What we do know

now is that selling successfully is only half of the task—the other half is to keep the business. Organizations spend millions of dollars annually to attract and sell new business. They then lose it for any number of reasons and must replace it. The saga continues.

Sales, as a career, is about finding good potential prospects who can benefit from your products or services, persuading them to buy from you, and then maintaining positive ongoing relationships with them to ensure repeat, referral business, as well as good references. Are you focusing solely on any one particular aspect of the sales process as you sell? Are you weak in any particular part?

Think About It

◆ ◆ ◆

To be successful, you must adjust your selling style to accommodate your prospect's buying style.

Each element of the process is inextricably related to the others. For example, consider prospecting. If you have a poor prospect, you will find it difficult to give a solid sales presentation. You will not be able to overcome the prospects' objections to the sale and as for closing the sale—forget it.

How about the issue of attitude in the sales process? Let's say you lack confidence in the quality of your products. That will affect your willingness to find new prospects. If you do find some, your lack of confidence will affect your ability to give a confident sales presentation.

What about one more issue? Let's say you have a fear of rejection. This will have an impact on your willingness to ask questions to qualify your prospects and discuss sales presentation issues that your potential clients might perceive as less than ideal. And asking for the order? Well, not in this lifetime.

I am sure you see my point. If you are going to sell successfully, you can't just improve one aspect of the sales process. You can't compensate for poor prospecting with tricky closes. You can't cover up your lack of knowledge of the product with fancy footwork.

Getting Ready to Sell

Selling today is easier, in many ways, than it was in the past, but in other ways it is more difficult.

It is easier because of the Internet, the globalization of business, improved customer education and sophistication, better quality products and services, improved organizational management, and increased training in sales skills.

At the same time, it is more difficult because of the Internet, the globalization of business, improved customer education and sophistication, increased consumer choices, organizational downsizing or restructuring, reduced layers of decision-makers, time compression, organization turnover, and product life cycles.

How, then, are the salespeople of today to survive, succeed, and excel? They can and should take multiple actions.

1. Develop positive sales rituals.
2. Develop emotional and psychological anchors that keep you focused.
3. Read some self-help material every day.
4. Study the competition.
5. Know your own products and services better than anyone.
6. Manage your time and territory effectively.
7. Maintain balance in your life.
8. Maintain your sales training either through your organization or on your own.
9. Develop career advocates.
10. Become a positive resource for your prospects and clients.

11. Keep asking yourself how you can improve.

12. Have clear, focused, and specific career goals.

13. Network with people who can help you.

14. Listen to self-help audiotapes in the car to and from work or on the way to appointments.

15. Develop strategic alliances in your career with people who can advance your career success.

16. Subscribe to and read publications that service your industry or those of your clients' and prospects' industries.

17. Develop daily, weekly, monthly, and yearly affirmations that motivate you to action.

18. Learn to relax, flow, and be—rather than push, manipulate, and control.

19. Become a solution creator for your clients rather than just a problem solver.

20. Cultivate your ability to communicate effectively: Improve your vocabulary, learn to speak in front of groups, and write effective letters and articles.

Why People Don't Buy

People buy for individual and personal reasons, not for the reasons the salesperson's (or the organization's) marketing department thinks that they should. You cannot turn a poor prospect into a customer with a great product or persuasive sales appeal. The key to increasing sales is to identify why people buy and what causes them not to buy. People don't buy for any number of the following reasons:

1. They can't afford what they want.

2. They don't really know what they want.

3. They have a generally poor history with salespeople or organizations.

4. They don't want the product or service.

5. They don't need the product or service.

6. They have not been convinced that the value equals the price.

7. They are concerned with what others will think of their purchase.

8. They don't trust the salesperson.

9. They don't trust the organization.

10. They don't like the product or service.

11. The timing isn't right for them to make the purchase.

12. They are indecisive buyers.

13. They don't trust the salesperson (repeated intentionally).

When a prospect doesn't buy, do everything possible to determine what prevented the purchase—especially if this was a well-qualified prospect. This can be done with a visit after you make the sales call, a telephone call, a letter, an e-mail, or a fax. Once you learn why many of your prospects are not buying, then, and only then, can you disarm these resistance areas during the sales process.

When a prospect doesn't buy, do everything possible to determine what prevented the purchase—especially if this was a well-qualified prospect.

Most ineffective salespeople give more information than they get. They *talk too much*. You learn nothing while you are talking. You can learn a great deal if you can get and keep the prospect talking. After every failed sales attempt, make it a regular practice to ask the prospect, "What was it about our product or service that prevented you from making a favorable decision?"

You will learn a great deal that can have a positive impact on future sales results if you consistently determine why people don't buy from you or your organization.

Competition for Thought

Let's say that you sell widgets. Your prospect can use more or better widgets.

On Monday, you present the features and benefits of your widgets to a new prospect. The prospect tells you he will consider purchasing them from you, but needs some time to consider your proposal.

On Tuesday, another salesperson who sells a totally unrelated product gives your prospect a presentation on the advantages of a new communication network system for his organization. No competition, right? Wrong! Although both of you are selling completely different products, you are both trying to get a share of the dollars that the prospect has

Who Are Your Competitors?

Salespeople tend to think of their competition only as organizations that sell the same products or services that they do. I would like you to see this issue from another perspective.

To sell successfully, then, you need to be better than every other salesperson who is trying to get some of your prospect's available cash—even though you don't know who your competition is or what they are trying to sell. Tough job? Not really. All you have to do is have better sales skills.

So who are your competitors? Let go of the attitude that they are only companies who sell exactly what you sell.

Clerk (Order-Taker) or Pro?

What is the difference between a clerk (an order-taker) in sales and a professional salesperson? I summarize the definition that I have used as follows: You go into a tire store to buy new tires, and they take your credit card and put on the new tires. Order-taker. You venture into a retail establishment, and you purchase a new dress or suit, and available to spend this year on a variety of products and services. The prospect calls you back on Friday and says that he has decided to purchase the communication program and can't order your widgets until next year. Lost sale. A direct competitor? *No.* You both were trying to earn some of the available financial resources of this prospect. He wanted and needed your widgets and the communication program both, but couldn't afford both now. An indirect competitor? *Yes.*

Apparently, the communication salesperson did a better job of convincing the prospect that he needed to buy the communication system than he needed to buy your widgets. He might not even have known the prospect was considering buying widgets, and you might not have known he was considering buying the communication system.

the clerk takes your check and puts your merchandise in a bag. Clerk. Not all tire-store or retail salespeople are clerks; this is only an illustration. Essentially, clerks take your money and put stuff in a bag.

How about a pro? You go into the same tire store or retail store and want to buy a new suit or tires. The clerk (salesperson) asks you several questions to ensure that what you are buying will satisfy not only the demands of your budget, but also your long-term expectations. Pros are more interested in solving your problems than selling you stuff. I don't care if you are selling ten-million-dollar airplanes or Amway soap. The criteria are the same.

Clerks generally make a modest wage. The pros can make a fortune. What's the difference? Here are a few of what I view as the important traits of professional salespeople today (and it doesn't matter what you sell, so don't sit there thinking, "I only sell a low-price consumable, or a seasonal item, or whatever.")

Sales Cycles

Many products and services have different sales cycles—from the first time the salesperson meets the prospect to the close of the sale.

Qualities of Successful Salespeople

As discussed throughout this book, successful salespeople have many attitudes and characteristics that contribute to their success. Effective salespeople also:

- Get more information than they give.
- Promise a lot and deliver more.
- Are interested in your satisfaction, happiness, concerns, and other issues.
- Are more interested in how you benefit than what they get in the form of compensation.
- Are really good listeners.
- Have the ability to ask good questions.
- Care.
- Want a long-term relationship.
- Sell value, not price.
- Give you outstanding service.
- Are an ongoing resource for their customers.
- Survive for the long term.

Can you add any? Go ahead—see if you can expand this list. Remember, a pro is not defined by what he or she sells, but how the sale is conducted.

Some cycles can last several months to a few years. Some can last only a few days.

Many salespeople believe that they are not in control of the sales cycle. They put the buying control into the hands of the prospect. Of course, you cannot sell something to someone before they are ready to buy, but you can discover the sense of urgency, or you can attempt to create it.

Keep in mind that people buy when they are ready to buy, not when you need to sell.

Let's focus on these arbitrary sales cycles. First of all, remember that you do not change the prospects' buying needs, timetable, readiness, or urgency—you discover it for them. If your prospect has just signed a three-year contract with a competitor, guess what? This is not a prospect for you until the time when he or she begins to consider renewing or changing suppliers.

Most sales cycles are not etched in stone. They are a function of your ability to get to the real issues, needs, pain, and problems. If you fail to identify these accurately, you will most likely never develop the interest or desire necessary to make a prospect decide to buy your product or service. However, if you are adept enough at questioning and can quickly cut to the chase of the prospect's primary emotional buying motive, and you respond to that motive well, you can most likely move the sales process along more quickly.

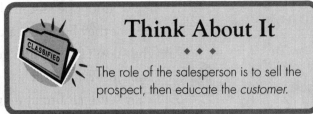

Think About It

◆ ◆ ◆

The role of the salesperson is to sell the prospect, then educate the *customer*.

Don't get yourself into the paradigm that your sales cycle always has to be eight weeks, six months, seven days, or whatever. Those of you who believe that your normal buying cycle is, let's say, six months, I'll bet that you have closed sales in less time than that. The point is that the cycle is not a predetermined period of time. It is a function of your ability to identify critical prospect issues and then show the prospect how you can satisfy these issues in a way that the prospect can accept.

This is also true of budgets. Budgets are generally not developed without flexibility. If the prospect has a pressing need or challenge that your product or service solves, trust me, they will find the money to pay for it. A game I love to play when I hear budget as an issue is: "Let's find the money. It has to be somewhere!"

Resist the tendency to fall into the budget trap—when the prospect says they need the product or service but lacks the money. If the money can't be found, the prospect probably does not need what you're selling very badly. So find another prospect. *Next*.

Maintain Control

One of the biggest mistakes that ineffective salespeople make is that they lose control of the sales process. They can accomplish this in many ways. Following are a few for your consideration:

1. They quote price—only because the prospect has asked (before they have had a chance to build value).
2. They don't ask enough questions early in the sales process. They just ramble on.
3. They send out literature when asked, without first verifying that the prospect is a good one.
4. They deliver proposals to the prospect's door and wait for an answer. To buy or not to buy, that is the question.
5. They fail to set appointments that are convenient to them, always bowing to the customer.
6. They lug equipment to demonstrate in the prospect's office rather than getting the prospect to visit their office.
7. They don't get deposits, but hope that the prospect will pay someday.
8. They leave "will calls" when telephoning a prospect.

I could go on but I am sure you get my drift.

Control is one of the key elements for success in sales. Successful salespeople understand that control is not manipulation, but is in the ultimate best interests of the prospect or client.

I bet you have a prospect right now, as you are reading this, with whom you have lost control.

I bet you have a prospect right now, as you are reading this, with whom you have lost control. You are waiting for this prospect to respond to your offer, appeal, or whatever. I know because I teach this stuff, and I am guilty, from time to time, of making the same mistake. How do you get and keep control? It is simple, but it is not easy. The best time to get control of the sales process with a new prospect is in the early stages of the relationship. It is very difficult, if not impossible, to get it back later if you don't get it early. One of the best strategies is: *Get information before you give it.* Questions should always come before your presentation, pricing, and literature.

Successful salespeople determine not only the buying habits and payment philosophy of the prospects and clients they have, but also the respect they receive and the manner in which they are treated by these prospects and clients. I have some great clients. Their behavior makes me want to do an even better job for them. I also have a few difficult clients. Guess what? They told me they were going to be difficult in the beginning, as well as in the early

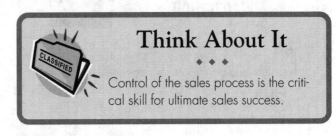

Think About It
◆ ◆ ◆
Control of the sales process is the critical skill for ultimate sales success.

stages of the relationship. Some of you may have some clients that you wish you didn't have. Right? Pay attention to early signals and remember: You and I have what our prospects want and need—solutions to their needs and problems. So keep control of the buying process.

Sales Questions

Accurate and timely information is the key to success in sales. One of the biggest mistakes ineffective salespeople make is that they give information before they get it. If you practice this approach, you are going to make one or all of the following mistakes. 1) You will give too much information (more than is necessary to make the sale). 2) You will give the wrong information (based on the prospect's needs, wants, desires, or problems).

Traditional sales training, for many years, has stressed the importance of the presentation, delivering your sales message, or closing the sale and getting the order. Unfortunately, these two elements are equally unimportant if you are not in the presence of a qualified prospect. Remember, your prospect will tell you what you need to tell them to sell them.

Preparation, Preparation, Preparation

There are a number of important reasons for developing a long list of questions that can be asked at various times during the sales process, such as to:

1. Gain control of the sales process. The person who asks the questions controls the conversation; the person who talks the most dominates it.
2. Capture and maintain the prospect's attention.
3. Build a positive rapport.
4. Save you time.
5. Help you avoid rejection.
6. Determine how cooperative the prospect will be.
7. Uncover potential sales resistance.
8. Prevent you from talking too much.
9. Determine the prospect's dominant emotional buying motive.
10. Help you determine the prospect's personality style and how to approach and work with it.

Keep in mind that information is power. I recommend that you spend more time planning the questions you are going to ask during your next sales visit than the information you are going to give.

The Skill of Asking Good Questions

The foundation for a positive sales outcome for both the salesperson and the prospect or client is the accuracy, amount, and timeliness of information.

It is difficult to give an effective sales presentation if you lack enough information on prospect wants, needs, concerns, issues, problems, or interests. It is difficult to close a poor prospect. Poor prospects tend to give more sales objections than well-qualified ones.

The most important sales skill that you need to master (to improve your sales results as well as customer satisfaction and loyalty) is the ability to ask well thought-out questions in an effective manner.

There are several types of questions, but the two we will address are open- and close-ended questions. Open-ended questions ask for feelings, opinions, interests, attitudes, history, awareness, and anything that gives information. Open-ended questions tend to encourage more dialogue.

Close-ended questions ask for specific information, or a "yes" or a "no." Close-ended questions tend to shut the dialogue down.

In every sales presentation, you need to ask close-ended questions as well as open-ended ones. Here is a strategy that I recommend. Start the presentation with open ones to get the prospect comfortable talking. When you ask a close-ended one, follow it with an open-ended one to get the conversation moving again.

In every sales presentation, you need to ask close-ended questions as well as open-ended ones.

Here is the opening question I have been using for more than thirty years. If it works for you, use it. "I don't know how I can be of service to you. The only way for me to determine that is if I can ask you a few questions. Is that okay?"

Increasing Referrals

It is easier, less stressful, less costly, and less time-consuming to sell to qualified referrals than any other source of prospects. It is amazing how many salespeople fail to make asking for referrals a regular part of their selling behavior. Getting referrals is not rocket science. Although there are several methods to generate referral business, the best way I know of is to just ask.

I have surveyed my sales audiences for more than twenty years by asking them how many would like to have more referrals. I always get a unanimous show of hands. My next question is, "Why don't you have them?" and the answer is always, "I don't ask."

Referrals can come from anywhere: from customers, noncompeting salespeople or suppliers, friends, your banker, neighbor, and even your relatives.

Referrals can come from anywhere: from customers, noncompeting salespeople or suppliers, friends, your banker, neighbor, and even your relatives.

There is no wrong time to ask for referrals. Many salespeople feel that to ask for referrals from customers, they must have first provided the service or product in a satisfactory way.

Why wait to ask? Every minute you are not creating a referral awareness in the minds of your customers or other sources, your competitors might be one step ahead of you.

Timing is important in selling. Every minute you lose discovering a new prospect that will benefit from your produce or service brings you closer to missing out on additional business.

Don't wait. There are several ways to generate referrals. You can call a customer, write them, fax them, or visit them for the sole purpose of asking for referrals.

Ingredients of Positive Sales Presentations

The attention span of the average adult is twelve to fourteen seconds. If your sales presentation lasts more than one minute, don't flatter yourself thinking that most prospects hear or remember what you say.

In a recent sales survey, it was discovered that most salespeople cover five to seven features during their presentation. When asked what the prospect remembered 24 hours later, they mentioned only one of the features. Guess which one? Not the first one, or the last one, but the one that related to their need, want, problem, desire, or concern.

So what is the key to an effective sales presentation? Only cover the features and corresponding benefits of the issues that are of interest to the prospect. People buy for their reasons, not yours. People buy based on emotions and then justify their buying decision logically. Therefore, a powerful presentation:

People buy for their reasons, not yours.

- Comes from the prospect's perspective.
- Is interactive.
- Is a conversation with an agenda.
- Blends a balance of emotional appeal and logical reasons.
- Is brief.
- Lets the prospect tell you what he or she wants and/or needs.
- Qualifies interest in the features as you move along.
- Tests the prospect's interest along the way with trial closing questions.
- Adjusts to the prospect's personality style.
- Is customized and tailored to each prospect.

Most salespeople go into what I call a "feature dump." Are you giving more information than you are getting? Most good prospects are ready to buy before they tell you. Just give them a chance, and they will help you sell them.

The First Fifteen Minutes

Was it a comedy? A tragedy? A monologue or a documentary? A hit? Or was the show canceled? We are not talking about the latest effort from Hollywood or New York, but your last sales presentation.

There are three ways to evaluate the success of any sales presentation. Let's continue for a moment with our movie example. Before the script finds its way to your local movie theater, there have been hours of planning and organization, preparation, and execution; then the actual filming.

The sales process is a series of relationships—not just personal relationships, but the relationship between the elements of the process.

In every profession there are these same three steps, whether it is a doctor preparing for surgery, a builder building a house or a parent planning the next meal. There is always some degree of planning, preparation, and then execution. The success of the outcome or finished product depends on the effectiveness of all three. The sales process is no exception.

The planning or organizing is the pre-call research, investigation, and general information gathering. The organization is deciding the strategy for the call—not planning the information that will be delivered, but rather the sequence of events. The execution is the what you say and do once you are in the prospects domain. The focus of this section is on the execution. However, it is necessary to cover some of the necessary key points that should have been addressed in the first two steps if the actual presentation strategy, dynamics, and outcome are to be understood and successful.

The sales process is a series of relationships—not just personal relationships, but the relationship between the elements of the process. The first element is your attitudes, perceptions of, beliefs on, values, and judgments about the sales process and their impact on every aspect of the process itself. This element, more than any other, will determine your success or failure in selling. The next element is prospecting—where you get information. Next is the sales presentation, where you give information and answer sales resistance; then comes the close; and finally, servicing the client for repeat and/or referral business. The success of the sales presentation is a function of your effectiveness in managing your attitudes and the timeliness and accuracy of the information you receive. We are going to assume that you have what you believe is a good prospect, and you are now in the prospect's office ready to begin. It's show time.

As I said earlier, there are two basic types of questions that you want to use in the early stages of the sales process. They are open- and close-ended questions. Close-ended questions are used to verify specific attitudes and get answers to specific information requests. For example, "What equipment are you currently using? Who is your present supplier?" Open-ended questions are used to query the prospect's feelings, attitudes, opinions, prejudices, and judgments. For example, "How do you feel about the service you are getting from your current supplier? What has been your experience with our type of product or service?" Remember, close-ended questions cut off dialogue and open-ended questions encourage dialogue.

Fifteen Minutes to Shine

"You have fifteen minutes to convince me that I should give you any more of my valuable time." Ever heard that? Well, you will. And if your prospect doesn't say it, you can bet they are thinking it.

Your goals or objectives of the first fifteen minutes are to:

- Build a positive rapport.
- Establish an atmosphere of trust and respect.
- Gain control of the sales process.
- Fill in the gaps of specific prospect information that you have not learned to this point.
- Confirm the accuracy of previous information gained.
- Uncover prospect prejudices, needs, desires, attitudes, opinions, problems, and potential resistance.
- Discover the dominant emotional buying motive.
- Determine the urgency and the prospect's willingness to proceed now.
- Determine whether you are in the presence of the decision-maker or to discover who the additional people are that should be involved.

A lot in only fifteen minutes, yes, but there is one selling skill than can accomplish all of these in the time allotted: The ability to ask the right questions in the right way at the right time.

Information is power. Questions help you prevent lost sales by getting you important information about your prospect before you "deliver" your sales message. They will help you focus on only those features that are of interest or concern to the buyer.

Generally speaking, you want to use more open-ended questions in the early portion of the sales process. If you use a close-ended question early, follow it immediately with an open-ended question. You want to get the prospect talking and you want to keep them talking.

Remember that the person who asks the questions controls the conversation and the person who talks the most dominates it. Which do you think is the most effective strategy?

This strategy accomplishes three critical things in the early part of the presentation. First, it gets you in control of the sales process and gives you permission to get as much information as you can and need early. Remember that the person who asks the questions *controls* the conversation and the person who talks the most *dominates* it. Which do you think is the most effective strategy?

Remember, your prospects are constantly asking themselves, "Why should I give this salesperson more time?" Questions keep them focused on their needs, problems, and concerns, and off of your products, features, and selling style. Second, asking questions shows the prospect that you are more interested in them than you are in merely selling something, anything, to them. Being more interested in your clients than you are in yourself is one of the best ways to build trust and rapport in any relationship.

Third, questioning helps grab and maintain their attention by breaking through their preoccupation with the many other issues with which they are dealing at the same time.

There are a few concepts that you should consider, however, before you continue with your presentation:

Never discuss price until you have built value. Price will always seem high if value is perceived as low. The way you build value is to relate the features and benefits of your products and services to the specific needs, desires, or problems of the prospect. You must first know what these needs, desires, and problems are before you can build value. If you introduce price too soon you will end up in a price-alone battle. An early request for a price is a signal that you have a poor prospect or one who will decide to buy based solely on price. The way to disarm a premature price request is to say something like, "I am sure price is a concern to you. Are you only interested in price, or are service, quality, and reputation also important to you?"

Don't deal in "maybes." I would rather leave early in the process with a "no" than go through the entire process and get a "maybe." When a prospect says "no," I know where I stand. With a maybe, I have only false hope. And after so many years in sales, my conclusion is that most maybes end up being no's. If you terminate an appointment, be sure to leave behind a prospect, not an enemy. One way to accomplish this is to say, "Mr. Prospect, your answers to my questions have indicated that this is not a good time to be discussing our product or service. Permit me to get back to you in six months to see how your circumstances have changed."

Timing is everything in sales. Remember, people buy when they are ready to buy, not when you need to sell. Attempting to force a prospect to buy when you need to sell is what we commonly call *the hard sell*. There must be a sense of urgency, or you must create one.

Back to the presentation.

Your opening question and those with which you follow up will determine how much more time your prospect will allow you. Ask poor questions, and you'll be out of there. Ask good questions, and you can stay as long as you must to determine whether you have a prospect who is worth more of your time. The critical thing to remember is that you are not selling your product or service in this early stage. You are earning the right to take more of your prospect's time later.

Let's relate this entire scenario to one that isn't as different as it might sound: visiting your doctor because you are having stomach problems. If the doctor prescribed a medication right after you informed him or her of your symptoms, I doubt if you would take that advice. Doctors need information, and they get it from a patient history, exam, x rays, and so on. Once a doctor feels confident that he or she sees the big picture, it's time to make a diagnosis—and you will be more receptive to that diagnosis, too. What if you arrived in the office and were told that the doctor would be willing to spend only fifteen minutes to decide your medical fate! I would bet that you would find another doctor. What if the doctor spent the entire time telling you about his or her education, experience, successes, personal philosophies, and other matters unrelated to your problem? You aren't there to hear that information. By the same token, this is not why you are in the prospect's office. You are there to obtain information, not to give it. You'll have time for that in the second segment of the sales process.

Let's summarize with a few basic sales rules.

1. Your prospects will tell you what you need to tell them to make the sale.
2. The information you don't learn soon enough will hurt you later in the process.
3. Merely because the prospect agrees to see you doesn't mean that he or she is a good prospect now.
4. People buy from people they trust, not people they like.

5. Your role is to sell the prospect then educate your customer, not educate prospects and sell customers.
6. You will never close a sale on a poor prospect with a good product, good sales presentation, or tricky close; however, a well-qualified prospect will help you sell them.

The first fifteen minutes of a sales presentation are like building the foundation of a house. Get the foundation right, and the rest of the construction will be successful.

Today's Sales Environment

Corporate consolidation and restructuring have salespeople scrambling like never before in the history of American business.

The game changes with regularity and uncertainty. Yesterday's decision-makers are today's researchers. Last week's stable relationship is no longer a sure thing. Buying committees, group purchasing organizations, and senior corporate executives are making decisions that were once delegated. It is difficult, at best, to navigate in the choppy waters of today's corporate environment. Everyone seems to want lower or better prices. Many client and customer relationships are in jeopardy.

The New Economy Balancing Act

How can today's salesperson balance the drive for corporate profits and the customer's desire or need for lower prices and high value without sacrificing the organization's ability to maintain market share, competitive position, and long-term success? In this chapter, I address three areas related to this question:

1. What is the root cause of or catalyst for the drive for better price?
2. What will the impact be if this better-price trend continues?
3. How can salespeople continue to be successful in this new arena?

What Is the Root Cause and Catalyst for the Drive for Better Price?

For the past several years, consumers have been effectively selling salespeople on the idea that price is their most important concern. At first, this attitude moved into business purchasing gradually, then accelerated to lightning speed. Purchasing agents have always been price conscious, often pitting one supplier against another to gain a better or lower price. This is not new behavior. But the zeal with which they are increasing this price shopping is taking a great toll on sales efforts in every industry.

Today, corporate buyers are putting increasing pressure on salespeople to give them better prices. Often the buyers sacrifice customer satisfaction and loyalty in this drive to lower their costs. These savings are sometimes not justified if you to look at the long-term market consequences. There may be short-term apparent savings off the direct bottom line, but sooner or later the real "costs" will become quite evident. These future costs can be in poor customer awareness, loss of competitive market position, or turnover of key personnel, to mention only a few.

Permit me to expand this idea a little further. There is low cost and low price. There is high or low value. And there is a fair price and cost for a good value. Consumers have proven again and again that it is the third that they want.

Price is what you pay for a product or service, and cost is what it ultimately costs you. I have discovered in the past twenty years, as a trainer and consultant to a wide variety of organizations, that companies can always find money to fix a problem, but they never had enough money to prevent it.

An Unhealthy Philosophy

The recent changes in purchasing practices in the health care industry are an excellent example of low prices equaling higher costs. The trend in this industry is to consolidate purchasing, with group purchasing organizations, thereby enjoying the benefits of lower costs because they can consolidate purchasing and thus improve their overall buying power. I believe that this drive for lower prices will ultimately hurt, not benefit, the customer or patient. Yes, it is true that many organizations need to become more efficient and prudent in their buying, as well as to rethink their profit objectives and margins, but to squeeze corporate America until it bleeds benefits no one.

Time and time again, I have seen corporate buying decisions made with little thought for how a marginal product or service would cost them decreased efficiency, loss of good reputation, and greater customer turnover in the future. Making purchasing decisions in which the only focus is cutting costs is shortsighted.

What Will the Impact Be if This Better-Price Trend Continues?

I am beginning to see a backlash in corporate purchasing in many industries. Increasing numbers of customers are now venting their disappointment, frustration, and anger with these organizations that have become penny-wise and pound foolish. And they are expressing their disapproval by taking their business elsewhere.

Organizations need to revisit their willingness to sacrifice the ultimate benefit of high value for the immediate pleasure of low price.

Another trend of these past few years, one that I've noted in various industries, is that decision-making is moving higher up the corporate hierarchy. For several reasons, I believe that this trend will not last:

First. With the thinning of management levels and staff in many organizations, the people at the top have more and more responsibility that often requires their immediate attention. For this reason, they will have neither the time nor the ability to make the best overall purchasing decisions.

Second. In the most successful organizations today, decision-making, authority, and autonomy is moving down the ladder, not up. The 1960s, 1970s, and most of the 1980s were dominated by a top-down management mentality. The employee rebellion of the late 1980s and early 1990s has cured that malady in most of the fast-growing and successful organizations of today. However, some organizations are refusing to modify their opinions, expectations, and business style. These organizations will soon find themselves far behind their competitors with no hope of ever regaining their lost market share.

Third. The best people to evaluate a product or service and its worthiness and value are the people who must routinely use the product or service. Often they are the point people—those who deal directly with your customers. Shoving inappropriate, poor quality, or outdated products and services down the throats of employees who must ultimately defend these to the customer causes increased stress, frustration, and fires the pilot light of discontent.

Fourth. History shows that saving money in the short term does not always mean saving money in the long term. You can't measure everything with a calculator or a spreadsheet. Saving a dime per widget when you buy thousands per month may cost a machine operator, customer service representative, or repairman excessive downtime. It will certainly take a toll on their attitudes and morale that will find its way to the customers' office, showroom, or plant.

How Can Salespeople Continue to Be Successful in This New Arena?

A number of factors contribute to the salesperson's decision to lower price or cave in to customer pressure and price demands:

First. There is the self-esteem of the salesperson. Salespeople with low self-esteem tend to reduce prices more often than salespeople with high self-esteem. This is because they hope to receive appreciation, approval, or recognition, all of which are psychologically necessary to them. Salespeople with high self-esteem are not looking for approval, but to make sales and solve customer needs, problems, or wants in both the short term and long term. They also tend to be much stronger negotiators for the same reasons.

Second. If an organization is losing market share, for whatever reason, they will tend to react by lowering prices, which only accelerates their demise or shortens their life span. It becomes a downward spiral. Increased competition leads to lower prices, which leads to less working capital to satisfy the organization's ability to compete, which results in less satisfied customers and increased customer turnover, which means less and less working capital, and so on, into oblivion. Exaggeration? Just look at the increased numbers of businesses of all sizes that have failed during the past several years.

Third. A corporate attitude prevails in many organizations today that says to get more business, you must give away more business. I have seen hundreds of organizations that have believed that to penetrate a new market or introduce a new product or service they had to "low ball" their products or services to get a foothold. I have never seen this work as a long-term strategy either for the organization or their customers. Both lose in the end.

Fourth. Many salespeople are price- or numbers-driven. Their mandate from is to increase sales at whatever cost. They are often successful in increasing sales, but at what cost? High stress, burnout, high turnover, and often at reduced margins. Not to mention dissatisfied, disloyal customers.

Fifth. Organizations need to price their products or services with careful consideration of the following:

- Is the product unique in the marketplace?
- Do customers really want what the company has available?
- Is the product quality less than, the same as, or better than the competitors' product?
- Is the market right for the product, or is the organization attempting to force a segment of the market to purchase what it chooses to design and manufacture?
- Is the organization pricing a particular product or service to make up for general corporate losses or because other items in its line are weak?
- Is sales compensation unfairly or poorly pegged to force salespeople to sell certain products or services that would otherwise be losers?

Now, back to our original question. How can today's salesperson balance the drive for corporate profits with the customer's desire or need for lower prices and high value without sacrificing the organization's ability to maintain market share, competitive position, and long-term success?

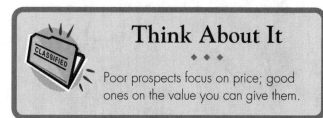

Think About It

◆ ◆ ◆

Poor prospects focus on price; good ones on the value you can give them.

I would like to share three simple yet proven strategies that can reduce and often completely disarm this "price-only" mentality among today's buyers. Salespeople need to have a number of things going for them to handle this price issue successfully. They must:

- Know a tremendous amount about their product.
- Know a great deal about their customers.
- Know the needs, fears, problems, concerns, or wants of their customers' customer.
- Have the skill to match their product knowledge to the needs, desires, concerns, and problems of customers.
- Have a "general basic business understanding."
- Bring a great deal of practical experience or empathy to the sales process.
- Have high self-esteem.
- Have exceptional sales skills.
- Posses the ability to manage the emotional issues in sales.
- Manage the issue of rejection.
- Believe in the mission, objectives, and purpose of their organization.

Tall order? Yes, but then the rewards can be just as big.

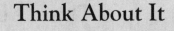

Think About It

• • •

People do not simply want the lowest price, even if they think they do. They want the best value for a fair price.

Now: the three strategies. For the purpose of brevity, I am going to assume that you have all of the above issues under control.

First strategy. If you believe that price is a major issue with your prospect or customer, you need to determine what else matters and why it matters. You can accomplish this by asking lots and lots of good questions in the right way at the right time. Do not, I repeat, *do not,* launch into your presentation before you've figured out what the prospect's dominant reason for buying is, other than price. Once you have discovered this, you need to focus on how your product or service addresses this reason. If the prospect attempts to control the sales process by bringing you back to price, you need to stand your ground and confirm whether this is his or her only consideration.

Keep in mind that buyers buy when they are ready and not when you need to sell. Also remember, they buy for their reasons, not yours.

Second Strategy. Resist the urge to quote price before building value. Price will always seem high if value is perceived as low. If you quote a price before you have attempted to establish a sense of value in the mind of the prospect, that price will seem high. You build value not by talking about product features or product benefits, but by highlighting product benefits and customer benefits.

Third Strategy. Don't be greedy. If you are dealing with a repeat customer who has a history of buying from you, don't jeopardize the business by an unwillingness to be flexible on some products, while not reducing prices on other products or services. The important thing to remember is that the person is your customer. There is a history with you and the customer is familiar with your service levels, response times, new product developments, and procedures for billing and shipping. When a customer asks you for a better price on an item, he or she may be looking for a lot less of a decrease than you think. Don't react too quickly. Ask why a better price is necessary on that particular product. Ask for something else in return if the customer asks you to reduce a price where you are not inclined to want to do so. Request advance payment, a bigger deposit, or perhaps a portion of the customer's business that you are not currently getting. But if you must take less than your desired margin, get something in return.

By asking for something in return, you can often stop the price spiral from continuing. You may even get some of their business that you might not have been able to do otherwise.

Price is important, but every survey I have seen in the past several years has indicated that buyers want three things: low price, good service, and good quality. Which do you think, again and again, comes up number one? If you guessed service, you are right. Which comes up number two? If you guessed quality, you are right again. That leaves price as number three. Price is important, but in the minds of most buyers, it is not the most important factor in their buying decision. They would like to convince you that it is, and often do, but never forget, most consumers and business buyers do not want to sacrifice service and quality for low price. They just want you to think that they will.

The Cost-Price-Value Issue

If I were to ask a room full of a thousand salespeople (I have done it) what is the number-one thing consumers want today, what do you think their answer would be? You guessed it—lower price. And second? Quality? Right again. And third? Service. Bingo. Now, let's switch scenes for a moment. I now have a thousand consumers or business buyers in my audience, and I ask them the same question. What answers do you think I would hear?

One of the most frequent answers I get is: first, service; second, quality; third, lower price. Well, folks, we seem to have a perceptual difference in what people want and what they tell salespeople they want. How can you account for that difference?

I believe it is for the following reason. It is a matter of definition. Price is defined as what we pay for something. We write a check, use cash or a credit card, and our account is debited.

Cost is what we pay for what we have bought over time. In other words, buy a cheap car, and you will have bigger service bills and inconvenience. You have a higher cost over time than the lower price you paid.

What do most consumers say they want—in your opinion? Yes, low price. But what do you think they really want? Yes, again, low cost. Therefore, it seems to me, we only need to question prospects better on what they really want and define the difference for them in terms of our product or service. What we are talking about here is value to the customer. And value is always "perceived" value. Every prospect interprets value in his or her own terms. Our job in sales is not to always lower the price (when that is often not the real issue), but try to better understand what the perceived value is for each prospect.

Think About It

♦ ♦ ♦

Sell the business on price and you rent the business. Sell it on value and you own it.

The only way to accomplish this is by asking constant, professional, and probing questions and then positioning your product or service appropriately in the mind of the prospect.

People don't want cheap. They want value. People don't really want things that rust, break, are inconvenient, or difficult to understand. They want life to be easier, less complicated, less stressful, happier, and more fun. Show them how your product or service can do all of these, and I guarantee price will never be an issue.

An Effective Closing Strategy

People don't like to make decisions. The main reason is that they prefer to avoid them is that they don't want to make a poor or wrong decision. Traditional sales closing methods ask people to make a decision. For example: Do you want it in green or red? (Alternative choice). Do you want to use your pen or mine? (Action close). Can we write up an order now? (Direct close). These closing techniques, even though they do work, have two fundamental problems. First, they ask the prospect to make a decision. Second, the average salesperson is uncomfortable using them.

Because people don't like to make decisions, I suggest you stop asking them to. Here is a simple close that I have been using for more than thirty years. Make the buying decision for the prospect and ask them to agree with the decision you have made. It goes like this. Let's do this, is that okay? Let's arrange for delivery on the fifteenth, is that okay? Let's get together on Thursday at 10A.M., all right?

This close works for three reasons. First, it gets a decision made, but the prospect doesn't have to make it. By agreeing with you, they, in essence, make the decision. I have found that people want to get decisions made, but don't want to make them. Second, it is common language. I guarantee in the next two to three days you will either say to someone or hear from someone, "Let's go to the movie, okay?" "Let's go out to dinner tonight, okay?" Third, then, the language is easy to remember and use, and it gets the job done.

When you use this close, the prospect only has three options. First, they go along with both your decision for them and your recommendation. Second, they go along with your decision, but don't like your recommendation. In both cases, you have a close. Third, they neither go along with your decision or recommendation. No sale. Keep in mind, though, that using this with a qualified prospect gives you a two out of three closing percentage.

This is the only close I have used for more than years years. Why? It works. Try it and find out for yourself. It can be used in any area of the sales process, from getting appointments to confirming sales.

Following Up On Lost Business

We all lose business—sales that are not closed, customers who decide to use a new supplier, businesses that no longer need our products or services, or any number of other valid reasons.

You cannot sell everyone and you cannot keep customers for life. It is a myth—no matter what you may have heard or read.

You cannot sell everyone, and you cannot keep the same customers for life. It is a myth—no matter what you may have heard or read. The key is to not lose them because of poor performance, poor quality, poor service, or poor sales skills.

Some salespeople, when they lose a sale or a customer, react irrationally in various ways: They blame someone or everyone, they make excuses, They sulk, they get angry, or they run and hide.

Successful salespeople understand the ebb and flow of business and relationships. If you have good sales skills, a good product or service, a positive attitude, and a good prospect, sooner or later you will sell them.

For certain, you will win some, and you will lose some. You won't win them all, and you won't lose them all. Just remember—staying power over the long haul is much more beneficial than short-term, quick success.

Reactivating Past Clients

Lost business does not necessarily mean that you have lost the client forever. Many salespeople neglect this lucrative source of new business. I say new because if you treat these past customers as new prospects, you may, in fact, regain the business.

Customers leave you for many reasons. Some of them are:

1. They no longer need the products or services that you sell.
2. They were wooed away by a competitor offering better prices, service, or some promise.
3. Management in the organization has changed, and they are not aware of the strengths of your services or products. Most likely, their predecessors did not pass this information on to them.

You Won't Win Them All

Here are a few suggestions to keep in mind when you don't close a sale:

1. Follow up with a thank-you note or letter.
2. Follow up with an after-sales critique or evaluation.
3. Follow up with additional sources, such as testimonials or articles, that offer independent positive opinions of the product or service that you sell.
4. Keep your prospects in an active follow-up file with regular contact by a newsletter, e-mail tip, or article that may be of interest to them.
5. Accept that things, people, and businesses change.
6. Find out what your competitor did better than you did to get the business.
7. Ask for feedback from prospects on what you could have done better or differently to earn the business.
8. Don't assume it was price if that is their sole explanation.
9. Don't let it negatively affect your attitude. Keep at it.

This week's lost business can be next month's sale. This month's lost customer can become next year's home run.

4. Your organization has outgrown an interest in them for any number of reasons, and they chose to begin again with a new supplier.

5. You or your organization failed to deliver as promised.

6. You or your organization let trust and/or respect erode in the relationship.

7. Your customers have outgrown your ability to deliver the products or services you provide.

8. There is some hidden agenda—they have a relative in the business, have lost buying authority, are leaving their organization for another position—some factor that you would have no way of knowing.

There are others, but most will fall under these eight. What can you do to regain this business?

1. *First, you must learn the real reason the customer left.*
   You and your organization must be willing to adjust or modify what you do, how you do it, or when you do it to convince the customer that it is in their best interests to rekindle the relationship.

2. *You have to be willing to begin again.*

3. *Work Harder.* It is important to remember that you need to work as hard to keep the business as you did to get it.

4. *You must reassess where you went wrong.* Was it a pricing issue, a service issue, a quality issue, a distribution issue, arrogance, ignorance, lack of interest in keeping the business, or some other major or minor mistake?

5. *You must keep in touch with previous customers.* You have many choices of how to do this: newsletters, direct mail, e-mail or conducting a lost business audit or critique.

The Value of Good Records

Have you ever experienced a sales slump? Or just not achieved the results that you thought you should have? Probably. Most salespeople have.

Successful selling requires many skills, attitudes, abilities, and personal values. When a salesperson experiences a down cycle in his or her success, it is impossible to look at only one area to determine where the problem is. For example, if you are having trouble closing sales, is it because you have poor closing skills, or could it be that you may be trying to close poor prospects?

Determining where the problem is, whether in a sliding sales career or a poor month, requires information. That information is about sales ratios, actual numbers, trends, and comparisons. It is difficult to take corrective action if you are not aware of what the cause of the problem is or what actions to take. Just working harder or longer hours calling on poor prospects is not going to have a significant positive impact on your overall results. You will only experience more of the same problems.

One of the common denominators (there are many) among top salespeople is their ruthless evaluation of activities, behaviors, results, and progress toward goals. Most ineffective salespeople don't take or make the time to keep accurate records. Many sales organizations require call reports, but those reports are, in many cases, no more than busywork. They provide little, if any, value for the salesperson or the sales manager about current or potential sales problems or their causes. They generally tend to require that you report whom you saw and

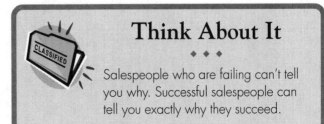

Think About It

♦ ♦ ♦

Salespeople who are failing can't tell you why. Successful salespeople can tell you exactly why they succeed.

what you sold. This is not enough information if you are going to reach the stars as a salesperson.

In my bestselling book, *Soft Sell*, the last chapter is devoted to which records to keep, how to evaluate them, and how to forecast the future based on the type and amount of your previous and current activity. If you are failing or doing poorly, do you know why? If you are consistently beating your goals, I will bet you have formed the habit of keeping good numbers and evaluating them on a regular basis to determine where you need to change your behavior or acquire new skills.

Answers to Remember

To summarize what I've said throughout this book, I end by sharing with you some of the questions I have frequently been asked by audience members during my twenty-five year sales training career. The answers are short—I will have more than likely covered many of the questions asked in the material in the first nine chapters of the book. What I do here is give you a few brief ideas to consider.

I have arranged the questions by topic area—attitudes, prospecting, presentations, time and territory management, sales objections, closing the sale, after-sales service, and administrative matters.

Take time to read through the following and figure out how you can apply these principles to your specific position. Remember these situations, answers, suggestions, and actions. Review them from time to time to make sure you continue to apply them in your career.

Attitudes

Question: How do I stay motivated in a down economy?

Answer: Motivation—real motivation—is inside-out, not outside-in. When you turn over the responsibility for your motivation to the economy, your boss, the weather, or any other outside influence, you have given up control of your most valuable tool—your mind. The best way to stay motivated inside is to have specific goals and

> *The best way to stay motivated inside is to have specific goals and keep track of your progress.*

keep track of your progress. Another thing I do is keep a "good stuff jar." Any time something good happens in my life or career, I write about it and put the paper in my jar. When things go sour, or I need a lift, I grab a few of the items in the jar and read or reflect on them. Trust me, it works. But it can only work if you put the stuff in when things are going well.

Question: How can I overcome a negative supervisor?

Answer: No one is perfect. Sooner or later you will have to deal with negative people: prospects, customers, fellow salespeople, your boss, or a friend or family member. Just keep remembering that *you* are the only person in charge of your attitudes, success, motivation, and feelings. Other people can't make you feel anything unless you allow them to do so. If you have a negative boss, you might try meeting with him and reminding him of how far you have come, how well you are doing, how much you have learned, and other positive aspects of your career. You have to learn to "blow your own horn."

Question: What is the best way to ensure I reach my goals?

Answer: There are four essential elements to reaching any goal. The critical factors: One, know why your goals are important to you. Just setting goals is not enough. You have to know *why* you want something. Two, write them down. Keeping your goals in your head is a sure recipe for failure. You need to be able to see them, change them, understand them, believe in them, and feel good when you achieve them. It is hard to do all that when they are only in your head. Three, give yourself deadlines. Don't give yourself forever to accomplish something. Remember, some goals require a lot more time to come to fruition than others. Four, reward yourself when you achieve a goal. Celebrate your success.

Reward yourself when you achieve a goal. Celebrate your success.

Question: Why are attitudes so important to my sales success?

Answer: Attitudes in life are everything. You do what you do, don't do what you don't, believe what you do, and don't believe what you don't because of your attitudes. Your attitudes are yours and only yours. When you let other people control your attitudes, you let them control your life. Attitudes come from feelings. Feelings are the result of habits. Habits are created because of values and beliefs. So what you believe will eventually come to pass in your life because your outer reality will become a reflection of your inner state of mind.

Prospecting

Question: What is the best way to get past a gatekeeper?

Answer: You need to keep multiple factors in mind. Confidence, belief, communication, and desire. Your confidence in yourself. Your belief in your products and services and how they will benefit the prospect. Your communication skills. And your desire to succeed. The role of the gatekeeper is not to keep you out but to shelter your prospects against people who will waste their time. The best way to get past this person (whether on the phone or in person) is to have the leverage of a referral or strategic alliance. These people can make it easier for you to get through to your prospect.

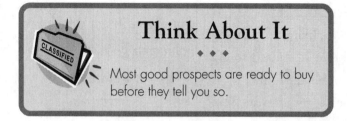

Think About It

♦ ♦ ♦

Most good prospects are ready to buy before they tell you so.

Question: How can I get to important decision-makers?

Answer: Decision-makers' time is very valuable. They don't want to waste it on poor or incompetent salespeople who have nothing of value to say or to offer. The best way to get through to a decision-maker is by way of a recommendation from someone they respect. Work at creating these types of relationships. It will take time, but in the long run, it will save you time by preventing you from spending extra time moving up through the channel to the ultimate decision-maker.

Question: How can I get more referrals?

Answer: The best way to get more referrals is to ask for them. This is not rocket science. But you first need to know who to ask. Referrals can come from anywhere: vendors, prospects, clients, personal relationships, previous customers, and even good old Aunt Sarah. The key is to understand what a good prospect is for you, then ensure that the referrals you get closely match that profile. In the end, though, the key to success with referrals is to ask more often.

Question: Is cold calling the most effective way to prospect?

Answer: In my opinion, cold calling is the least valuable use of your prospecting and sales time. Yes, yes, I know that many companies want their salespeople to spend endless hours cold calling. The reason is that they don't know how to teach them how to prospect more effectively. That being said, though, I do acknowledge that you have to have someone to sell to. When you begin your career, if you don't have referrals, strategic alliances, or are not effective yet at networking, then guess what—it's time to hit the streets. But, please—after you have been selling for several months, stop spending your valuable sales time using this ineffective method.

Question: How do I know when I have a good prospect?

Answer: Good prospects are everywhere. You just have to know where to look. The key to knowing whether you have a good prospect is to know the following: Is there a sense of urgency? Do they match your ideal customer profile? Is the timing right? Will they see you? Do they have a positive relationship with your competitor? Can you get to the final decision-maker? Do they really need, or will they benefit from, your product or service? Do they have the money?

> *Good prospects are everywhere. You just have to know where to look.*

Sales Presentations

Question: How long should a good presentation be?

Answer: As long as it takes to ensure that you have effectively gained your prospect's trust, confidence, respect, and willingness to buy. It also should not be longer than necessary. Most salespeople spend too much time in the presentation trying to talk the prospect into buying. People buy when they are ready. The purpose of the presentation is to give them enough information so that they will make a purchase. Then your job is to educate them on everything else you didn't cover. Some presentations can be as short as fifteen minutes, while others can take several meetings that may last a few hours each.

Question: What should I do if there is more than one person in the presentation?

Answer: This answer could fill an entire book. But here are a few things to consider. Don't play to any one individual. Don't ignore anyone. When you ask questions, look at each person for a response. Don't make assumptions as to who is the decision-maker. Encourage everyone to participate. Make sure everyone can see you clearly.

Position yourself so no one can look at a fellow member of the group without you being able to see their expression.

Think About It

♦ ♦ ♦

The critical factor in the sales process is control. Get it early, keep it, and don't ever give it up.

Question: What should I do if the prospect tries to rush me?

Answer: Poor prospects want you to get to the end of the sales presentation or process quickly so that they can be rid of you. Good prospects want you to know whatever you believe you need to know so you can feel confident that you can help them with their problem, challenge, or issue. Poor prospects are only concerned about the price and not the value. If the prospect tries to rush, you ask them a simple question. "You seem to be rushed. Should we reschedule this appointment when you will have more time?" If they won't reschedule, and you still feel you are being rushed, you might want to consider terminating the appointment. Here's how I do it. "Mr. Prospect, based on some of the answers to my questions, I feel this is not the best time for us to be considering doing business together. Permit me to get back to you (next week, month, year) to see how your circumstances have changed." But I am outta there. Remember, leave a prospect behind, not an enemy.

Question: How many presentations should I give before I give up on a prospect?

Answer: The mind of a prospect must go through four psychological stages: Attention, interest, desire, and action. My personal feeling is that it shouldn't take more than one presentation (appointment) for each of the four stages. So my limit is four.

Time and Territory Management

Question: How should I decide which new prospects to see in my territory?

Answer: This depends on a number of factors. How big is your geographic territory? What is the mix of A, B, and C prospects? How many active customers do you have? How much time can you allocate to field time? How many maintenance customers do you have? How much service time do you need to service existing customers? How complicated is your product or service? What is the typical sales cycle of a new prospect from the first visit to a closed sale? Do you need field support from other employees? How do you travel through your territory—car, air, or some other form of transport? Does your territory include more than one time zone? I know, a lot of questions, but no question is really that simple. As a general rule, you should make this decision with three factors in mind. First, make sure you spend adequate time with your best customers and prospects. Second, travel during non-sales time when possible. Third, don't spend too much time with poor or small prospects.

Question: How do I handle a customer or a prospect who takes too much of my time?

Answer: Every prospect or customer has unique demands for your time, information, after-sales service, and hand- holding. Some believe they need more of your time than is really necessary, while others have the attitude, "Don't call me unless there is a new product, service, or solution that I need to be aware of." These people still deserve your attention. It is the smaller or more demanding prospects and customers who steal your valuable time. The best

It is the smaller or more demanding prospects and customers who steal your valuable time.

way to handle this is to set up a regular schedule (not that frequent) to visit with them. Or you can handle them strictly on the telephone or with e-mail.

Sales Objections

Question: How do I overcome price objection?

Answer: Price is never the only issue. People usually object to price when their perceived value is low. The strategy here should be to discover where they have a lower perceived value, therefore contributing to the reason they won't justify your price. There are two things you can do here. One, determine if it is really a price issue by asking them how much is it worth to get their problem solved or need satisfied. Two, get back to selling value—what the product or service means to them. Recognize that there is a difference between price (what you pay for something) and cost (what it costs you to do it wrong, not at all, too little, or too late). Most prospects say they want a low price, when what they really want most of the time is a low cost. The key is to get their focus off of price and on to the cost. Resist the tendency to reduce price at the first sign of price resistance.

Think About It

• • •

When you encounter price resistance, it is best to sell value first, before you reduce or discount your price or terms.

Question: How do I overcome the objection that there is no rush to buy?

Answer: A sense of urgency on the part of prospects is often a critical aspect of a successful sales outcome. This urgent need or desire will often reduce their need for a low price, inadequate features, delivery issues, or other factors. If a prospect does not have a sense of urgency, you need to create it in a professional way. The way to do this is to focus on the prospect's problem, concern, need, crisis, or whatever. By keeping their attention on the concern and not on the product or service, you can greatly enhance the sense of urgency or the need to take action sooner rather than later.

Question: How do I overcome the "satisfied with my current supplier" objection?

Answer: The key here is to find a relationship between a need or desire they have and the inability of their current supplier to satisfy it. You accomplish this with targeted questions such as: "If we could do one thing better than your current supplier that would improve your satisfaction, what would that be? If we could offer you one feature or service that would be important to you that your current supplier does not offer, what would that be?" Avoid saying anything negative about a competitor. When you do, you indirectly invalidate their previous decision. Your prospect made a decision based on what he or she felt was sound judgment to do business with a competitor.

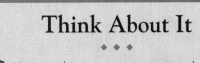

Think About It

• • •

You must know your competition: their strengths, weaknesses, goals, policies, and strategies.

Closing the Sale

Question: How early in the presentation should I attempt to ask for the order?

Answer: You are not a professional visitor. You are there to sell. If the prospect thinks your purpose is to educate them on the latest technology, choices, or whatever, then you have created the wrong environment. You and I both earn the same income on the sales we don't make—nothing, zilch, nada. You are there to help them solve a

> ## Think About It
> • • •
> Tailored, brief sales presentations are far more effective than feature-based, overloaded, and lengthy ones.

problem or take advantage of an opportunity, and you deserve the business if you can do either. The time to start closing is in the first minute. I don't mean you should ask for the order in the first sixty seconds, only that your attitude should be: I am here to do business. The best time to formally start the closing sequence is when the prospect asks for the price, gives you a buying signal, or asks a question like: How long will it take to get it? How long will it take to get the process started? What is the next step?

Question: What is the best way to close the sale?

Answer: The best close is when the customer buys. Problem is, if you wait for them you will most likely make very few sales. People like to buy things, but they don't like to make the decision to buy things. The key is to have them believe that they are buying when you are really selling. This is a professional and effective way to handle the close of the sale. You do not force, make, push, or in any way coerce anyone into buying before they are ready, but once they are ready, you need to take control of the buying process. I show you how to do this very effectively in chapter 9, so I won't waste paper here repeating myself.

Question: What do I do when a customer cancels an order on a sale I just made?

Answer: Get back with them in person immediately. Start with questions. You need to discover why they bought in the first place and what has changed since they made the buying decision. Has there been some negative outside influence from their supervisor? Are there some politics going on that you don't know about? Go back over the benefits of why they purchased: what they liked, how it solved a problem, answered a need, and anything else you'd discussed with them.

After-Sale Service

Question: How much time should I spend servicing my customers?

Answer: Time with customers depends on the situation. How much of their business are you currently getting? How much more business is there to get? Is a competitor beating on their door for the business? Do they give you lots of referrals? Are they a good reference for you? Is it a new customer? Is it your biggest customer? Your smallest? Your most difficult?

Question: How do I tell small customers they are using too much of my time?

Answer: Tell them to buzz off! Seriously, your time is the only asset you have. It is the one common denominator among all people—successful or otherwise. If you have customers who waste your time, the best technique is to schedule appointments or meetings with them on late Friday afternoon or early Monday morning. Why do you think these are the two best times to see these people? Tell them before you begin that you have a conference call scheduled in ten minutes, or that you have to get back to the office for an important meeting with your boss.

If you have customers who waste your time, the best technique is to schedule appointments or meetings with them on late Friday afternoon or early Monday morning.

Question: What is the best way to service a new customer for repeat business?

Answer: Deliver on your promises. One of the biggest weaknesses of poor salespeople is that they can sometimes do a good job of selling, but then drop the ball when it comes to delivering on what they promised.

Sales Records

Question: Why are sales records important?

Answer: They can help you spot potential future weaknesses. They can improve your sales results. They can help you accurately track your sales time and activities. They can help you identify strengths and the contributors to your success. They can give you benchmarks. They will help you increase your income.

Question: Shouldn't my manager's sales-call report be enough information to keep?

Answer: No. The typical call report required by management is designed to ensure that you are working, not necessarily that you are effective. Your success is far too important to leave your future up to a few basic sales statistics. If your call report is more thorough than the average, so be it. But I would bet that when you read my answer to the next question that it doesn't ask for even a fraction of my list below.

Question: What sales records should I keep?

Answer: There is no simple answer to this. Here's a list of a few of the important items. There are many more but these will get you started:

- Average income per sale.
- The ratio of telephone calls to appointments.
- The number of closed sales to appointments.
- Your average sales cycle time.
- The average number of referrals per customer.
- Average sales volume.
- Average number of sales per week/month/quarter.
- Percentage of business from current customers versus new prospects.

- The source of your best new prospects.
- Average length of a successful appointment.
- Average number of appointments to get a closed sale.
- Average volume of your first sale on a new prospect.
- How many new prospects you need per year to reach your desired sales results.

See how many more you can add to this list.

Administrative Matters

Question: How do I tell my boss that paperwork is wasting too much of my time?

Answer: I wouldn't make an issue out of it if you are really new or not doing well. This can be a touchy one depending on the attitudes of your boss, how new you are, and how successful you have been to date. You need to get leverage if you want to break some of the rules or policies. The best way to get leverage is through success. So get some sales under your belt. Hit a few home runs. Beat your quota, sell more than anyone else in the company, and then have a chat with your boss.

Beat your quota, sell more than anyone else in the company, and then have a chat with your boss.

Question: How do I avoid meetings that waste my time?

Answer: Well, it depends on who is holding them. If it is a meeting with your boss or your best client or prospect, good luck. If it is a meeting with another department or a fellow salesperson, you can always be busy somewhere else. Use a little creativity and finesse. Just tell the people who want the meeting that you can do it, whenever. When is whenever? It is when you want to see them and is most convenient for you.

Question: When is the best time to do paperwork?

Answer: Prioritize. As mentioned earlier in this book, you must break your time into two major areas: Prime Time and Prime Time Plus. Prime Time is when you are at your best—early morning, late in the afternoon. Your Prime Time Plus are those times when you are at your best and your prospects can see you. Paperwork and administrative responsibilities should be done during non-Prime Time and non-Prime Time Plus.

Appendix 1 _____

Act Now!

The key to sustained motivation in life and sales success is the ownership and mastery of basic skills and attitudes. With a guiding philosophy of learning, testing, integration, application, and reevaluation of skills, you are assured success as you pass through the stages of your life. With this approach, you will also have the ability to use these techniques and maintain attitudes with confidence—regardless of what new circumstances or conditions present themselves as you move through the natural ups and downs, successes and failures, and wins and losses in your career and life.

These assignments are designed to help you develop mastery in the critical attitude and skill areas necessary for sales success. Whether this is your first sales position or you have been selling for a few years, it is critical that you practice, integrate, and apply the lessons you learn. The following assignments will facilitate that learning process.

The assignments are in no particular order of importance. Each assignment, when completed, can have a dramatic impact on your overall motivation, confidence, and sales success. Give each exercise the time, effort, and commitment it deserves. Don't short-change your success by thinking that one exercise is less important than another. Once you have completed all of the exercises, I guarantee that you will see a tremendous improvement in your ability to sell more and enjoy greater success and lifestyle.

I recommend one to two weeks for each assignment, but you should give each what you feel necessary to ensure mastery, continued application, and ultimate success. It is likely that in less than one year you will have completed all of the exercises. This is a programmed strategic approach to your skill and attitude development rather than a hit-and-miss, slip-shod philosophy which will only add to your frustration, lack of success, and possible failure. Don't risk it.

There is one investment you must make to bring these assignments to life. Purchase a three-ring binder and a tab for each assignment and a ream of lined paper (cost: under $15.00) at your local office supply store.

I also recommend that you not complete any of the assignments until you have completed the text portion of the book. This information will allow you to get the most out of the exercises.

Good luck.

Attitude Management

Attitude in life is everything.

Make a list of five: regular customers, associates, friends, relatives, and suppliers or vendors. Ask each of them to describe your sales attitudes—positive and negative. List these twenty-five people in section two of your binder and leave room next to their names for their comments. After you have completed the interviews and recorded their feedback, review it looking for: similarities, incongruencies, areas for possible improvement, areas where you have blind spots, and areas where your self-perception was the same as others' opinions.

Purpose

All success is the result of a definite major purpose in life. You won't achieve all of your goals as long as you continue to reach for new heights, unless you set your goals very low. Purpose drives you forward regardless of the setbacks, problems, disappointments, and failures in your life.

1. *Define your driving purpose in life in twenty-five words or less.*
2. *Determine where you tend to give in or give up easily or early.*
3. *If they wrote a book about your life, what would the title be? What would the titles of the current chapter be? The next chapter?*
4. *How do you want the book to end?*

Start a Journal

A journal will become one of your most valuable possessions as you travel through the days and years of your life. A journal is a record of your successes, defeats, personal development, philosophy, goals accomplished, and goals abandoned. It is a written record of your life's peaks and valleys, lessons learned, and lessons yet learned.

Start a journal today. You already have a head start—you can use your binder as your journal. Just add sections to it as you move through the various stages of the rest of your life.

Control Your Thoughts

There is one trait that separates humans from every other species—the ability to control thoughts. It is interesting, however, how few people effectively exercise this ability. Most people let circumstances, other people, fears, and any number of outside issues influence and even control their thoughts moment-in and moment-out.

1. *Keep a journal of the recurring dominant thoughts that fill your mind: when you are upset, happy, frustrated, afraid, and confident.*
2. *At the end of each week for two weeks summarize those thoughts that kept popping up—whether positive or negative.*
3. *Develop a mantra or sentence that you can repeat over and over again when certain negative thoughts fill your mind.*

Desire and Belief

Desire is the beginning of all success. Purpose, plans, goals, and actions are a consequence of desire. What you vividly desire and believe will come to pass will one day be a reality. Belief is the second cousin to desire. If you can imagine it, believe it is possible, and create a burning desire for it, all that is required for success is consistent and purposeful action.

1. *What is your single, driving desire; the one thing that you want more than anything else?*
2. *Write it out as a statement as if it were already true.*
3. *Re-read that statement until you can state it from memory. Etch it on your very being, believe you deserve it, and watch the world help you move toward it.*

Manage Adversity

Everyone faces adversity in his or her life. No one escapes without some type of disappointment, failure, or significant life or career challenge. Each of us can determine if and how we respond to these trials. We can whine, complain, quit, try again, find a different approach, and any number of other positive and negative responses. Adversity has value only if we use it to get better, smarter, stronger, or more humble.

1. *List all of the major adversities you have had in your life to date.*
2. *Write down your reactions to them.*
3. *Do you see any patterns or recurring themes?*
4. *How would you like to learn to respond?*
5. *What is standing in your way of responding the way you wish—your belief system, expectations, values, self-esteem, attitudes?*

Motivators and De-Motivators

Some things motivate, others do the opposite.

In your assignment one (tab one) section of your binder, create two sub-sections:

1. *Things, people, and circumstances that motivate you to action.*
2. *People, things, circumstances, etc., that de-motivate your actions.*

Now turn to each section and create the following columns:

1. *Event/person/circumstance/date/your reaction/hindsight.*
2. *Complete the first three columns daily for at least two weeks.*
3. *Each week review your notes and complete the last column—hindsight (what you learned).*

Now create a third section:

List what you need to do/think/feel differently to improve your success. Spend time and put down some ideas on this subject.

Resonance

Each of us resonates out to the world a reflection of our values, beliefs, expectations, attitudes, fears, needs, and much more. With our words, tone, and demeanor, we say to the world: I like me, I don't like me. I like my job, I don't like my job. I am glad to be able to help you. I wish it were Friday and I was off work. There are many more examples I could give.

1. *For two weeks, ask a coworker whom you trust and respect to give you feedback on your attitudes, actions, and communication. Give permission to be honest; assure that you won't get defensive.*
2. *Audiotape your side of telephone conversations with customers and ask a different coworker to give you feedback on your tone and attitude.*
3. *Get a mirror and observe your facial expressions for one week while on the phone.*

Focus

Listen to your innerself talk. People bring into their lives *more* of what they focus or concentrate on. This inner-self talk, depending on whether it is positive or negative, will contribute to your behavior as you travel through life. We can focus on what is working in our lives or what isn't, what we have or is missing, and what we can or can't do.

1. *For one week, record your self-talk in your binder in the section marked Focus. Keep an accurate record of those topic areas where you tend to spend time and energy thinking either positive or negative thoughts about yourself, customers, fellow employees, life, or other people and things.*

2. *At the end of the week, summarize those common areas and see if you can determine how the thought pattern or focus is impacting the quality of your life, unresolved issues, and anything else.*

Old Baggage

Identify yours, deal with it, and move forward. Everyone has unresolved emotional baggage from the past. This old baggage, if not dealt with, can negatively impact your success in several ways. Thus, you need to confront it.

1. *Create a list of those emotional hurts, slights, and things that people have said or done to you, or not said or done, that you feel they should have.*

2. *Identify which ones are causing you continued stress, frustration, or emotional pain.*

3. *See if you can identify your expectations, feelings, or reasons why you still carry this baggage.*

4. *Identify which customers have the ability to push your buttons and cause you to respond negatively out of past attitudes or future expectations.*

It is important, as well, to remember to not let other people's emotional baggage become our destiny.

Personal Development

Your continued personal development is a *must* if you are to succeed in your career in sales as well as life.

1. *Spend a day in the library or your local bookstore. Find three books you feel will help your career, motivation, or success. Check them out or buy them.*

2. *Spend one hour a day for the next two weeks listening to self-help tapes and/or reading the books you selected in the bookstore or library. Don't just read or listen. Get in the habit of making notes as you read or listen. Put the notes in your binder in the section for this assignment. Now continue this habit after the two weeks have ended.*

3. *Spend five minutes every day thinking about how your personal development will contribute to your career success.*

Overcome Your Fears

Confront your fears and you will overcome them. Avoid them and they will continue to control your thoughts, actions, and life outcomes. Everyone has fears at some point in their life: the fear of heights, snakes, death, failure, success—yes, even success.

1. *List all of your fears.*
2. *Prioritize them in order of the biggest to the minor ones.*
3. *See if you can determine what you are really afraid of.*
4. *Ask yourself: What is the worst thing that can happen if I fail or confront my fear?*

Dream Big Dreams

Anyone who has ever accomplished anything of value has had a dream. Dreams are the stuff of hope, desire, and challenge. They pull us forward as they help us overcome obstacles and the negative people in our lives who try to discourage us.

1. *Ask yourself, "What would I try if it was impossible to fail—my success is assured?"*
2. *Write down all of your dreams that you would like to accomplish during the rest of your life (not goals—dreams are bigger).*
3. *Have you given up on any dreams because of age, health, or other people?*
4. *Why?*

Take Risks

No one can get out of this life without taking a few risks. To live life to the fullest requires "going for it" every once in a while—whether it is a new hobby, new career, or just going on vacation without making reservations. (I know, I know. Some of you just cringe at the thought.)

1. *Create a list of all of your fears (private and public, major, and minor).*
2. *Now prioritize them, putting the smallest ones at the top of your list and the biggest ones at the bottom.*
3. *With each one on the list, ask yourself, "What am I afraid of?"*
4. *Start with the smallest one at the top and just go for it.*
5. *Continue down the list (no matter how long it takes), going for it and building confidence and self-belief.*

Build Your Self-Esteem

Self-esteem and a healthy self-image are a must. Do you like you? Do you accept you and your life as valuable? Do you feel worthwhile? Or, do you only feel good when you are accomplishing, getting positive feedback from others, or succeeding? A healthy self-image or self-esteem is one of the most critical factors for success and happiness.

1. *Create a list of everything you like about yourself.*
2. *Now expand the items. Write a paragraph about why you like each specific trait or attitude.*
3. *Create a list of all of your accomplishments. Go as far back in your life as you can.*
4. *Ask people who know you well and like you to describe all of your positive attributes.*

Manage Your Stressors

Stress is normal. Every day there are positive and negative stressors in your career. The ultimate impact of stress is how you manage it "inside-out." The consequences of not managing stress in a positive way can be anything from physical illness to emotional withdrawal.

1. *Start a stress log.*
2. *For two weeks, every time you feel your body sending you stress messages—nervousness, anxiety, frustration, negative self-talk, loss of energy, etc., record the date and time, the symptoms, what you believe is the cause, and your reaction.*
3. *At the end of the two weeks, spend some time looking for common causes, consistent reactions, and their outcomes—how did they impact your life?*

4. *Create a list of all of the customers (or types of customers) you interact with who cause you the most stress. Ask yourself—what is it about these people or these relationships that is causing me stress?*

Planning

The key is to make plans and then embrace the unexpected. Nothing worthwhile will happen in your life that leaves a lasting sense of satisfaction and inner peace except those events, activities, and projects which have been carefully planned. Not all of your plans will work out, however, as you expect—that's life.

1. *Develop a planning template that you can use in your personal life and career. What should be included? Time frames, expected outcomes, available resources, possible obstacles, goals, and short-term action steps. Can you add any?*
2. *Apply this template against any current project or activity.*
3. *Follow the steps and record both successes and failures.*
4. *Reevaluate your template and make modifications where necessary to ensure success next time.*

Time Management

You can't manage time. You can only manage a variety of elements in your life as time passes.

1. *Create a list of your personal common time-wasters (activities that may be sabotaging your success).*
2. *Evaluate/estimate how much time you actually spend in each of these activities in a week. Record this information in your binder under assignment three.*

3. *Keep a daily log for two weeks in half-hour intervals. Log in how you spent that time: driving, reading the paper, solving problems, etc. At the end of the week, total the time in all of the major categories. Now the fun part—evaluate where you are wasting time and determine common time management habits that must be changed.*

Territory Management

You only have so much time to sell. Spending time with poor prospects or traveling during peak selling time is a certain career killer.

1. *Take the number of miles you drive in any given week and divide it by the number of sales calls you make. That number is your territory call effectiveness. See if you can lower that number with better call scheduling.*
2. *Now evaluate your per-call success (closed sales, average sales volume, or income) in that same week.*
3. *How can you increase that success? Better prospecting? Less wasted time with poor prospects? Better sales results—with higher sales-close ratios? Spend time evaluating how, where, and why you are not achieving the success in your territory you feel you are capable of. Then develop some new approaches to see more or better prospects with less wasted time and energy.*

Effective Networking

It isn't who you know, but who knows you. If you are not currently involved in groups that can increase your contacts and accelerate your career, what are you waiting for?

1. *Make a list of everyone you know who can contribute either to your personal growth or success. Call them and ask for their help. (It will be helpful to know what you want from them before you call.)*
2. *During the next two weeks, go out of your way to make at least one new contact a day.*
3. *Create a list of your top twenty-five advocates (people who are interested in your success). Cultivate this list regularly.*

Be a Resource

Competitor-proof your client relationships by becoming a better resource. This is also the best way to take prospects from a competitor.

1. *Call your top fifteen clients and ask them how you can be a better resource for them.*
2. *Call your top fifteen prospects and ask them the same question.*
3. *Talk to at least ten salespeople you know and ask them how they are a resource for their customers.*
4. *By now you should have a fairly extensive list of actions you can take to become a better resource. Select those areas where you have the time, expertise, and resources and create an action plan to begin being a better resource.*

Effective Communication

Effective communication is the glue that holds all relationships together. There are many ways we communicate, and good communication is more than the sharing of words or gestures—it is shared understanding, though not necessarily agreement. How you communicate on the phone or in person says a great deal about your self-image, confidence, attitudes, and ability to express yourself accurately.

1. *Make a list of your favorite words and then record how often you use them.*
2. *Learn a new word every day for the next two weeks.*
3. *Make a list of words that people use that you do not know the meaning of, and then look them up in the dictionary.*

Listening Skills

Not listening to a customer is one of the best ways I know to invalidate a customer. Most people don't listen well. I am not referring to hearing problems. Listening takes place on a mental level, while hearing is a physical act. Learn to be a great listener.

1. *The next several times you have dialogue with customers, ask them to paraphrase the thoughts you communicated to them.*
2. *In every conversation you have with a customer for the next week, focus on their intent or meaning, not just the words used.*
3. *With every conversation you have for a few days, write no more than a three-sentence summary of each conversation. Pay particular attention to assumptions made, expectations not verbalized, or words or ideas that cause your mind to wander.*

Common Customer Complaints

Perfect doesn't exist in the real world. Sooner or later you or your organization will disappoint a customer, perhaps even your best one. This doesn't mean you shouldn't try to give exceptional service every day, every time, to every customer.

1. *List the most frequent customer complaints you hear about your: organization, products, services, policies, and procedures.*
2. *Now prioritize the list. What are the most frequent ones?*
3. *Which ones do you have the responsibility or authority to impact?*
4. *Which ones need to be addressed higher up in the organization?*
5. *Take both lists to your supervisor and have a discussion about them.*

Conflict and Perceptions

Life is a perceptual experience. People look at everything through their own unique experiences, expectations, and feelings. No one is ever wrong—people just see things differently than we do. Most conflict in relationships comes from these unique and differing perspectives.

1. *What are some common perceptions your customers have of your: products/services, organization, and industry?*
2. *What are the biggest sources of conflict between your customers and your organization?*
3. *The next time you have a conflict with a customer, see if you can see the issue through your customer's eyes.*
4. *In hindsight, what could you have done differently to disarm the conflict?*

What Customers Want

Customers want many things: freedom from inconvenience, fair prices, effective follow-up, employees who care, quick response time, their problems solved—to mention just a few. Most customers, however, will settle for just three and continue to do business with you. They primarily want to be cared about, to be listened to and understood, and respected. Satisfy all of their needs and desires and you will own them forever.

1. *Create a list of those services/benefits/attitudes that you believe your customers want more than anything else.*
2. *Now create a list of all of the services and benefits that you deliver most of the time.*
3. *Is there an inconsistency in the two lists? If so, what can you do about it?*

Develop Strategic Alliances

Let other people help you sell. From clients, friends, and other salespeople who are in a position to help you accelerate the sales process and your results, there are numerous allies for you to utilize.

1. *Make a list of the top fifty people you know who could in some way contribute to your success.*
2. *Meet with each of them as time and logistics permit and ask them for their help, such as with names, resources, information about clients/prospects, etc.*
3. *Cultivate an active working relationship with as many of them as possible.*

Go the Extra Mile

Successful salespeople promise a lot and deliver more. Poor salespeople promise a little and deliver less. Going the extra mile means doing more for your customer than they expect, want, pay for, or need.

1. *Create a list of activities and services you can provide your customers to help them. This is not about helping them so they will*

buy more from you, but helping them build their business and careers. In other words, what can you give them—ideas, information, services—that will contribute to their overall success?

Study the Competition

Product knowledge is vital for your success. It is also critical that you know everything possible about your competitors.

1. *Go to your binder and make a list of all of your competitors.*
2. *Prioritize them in the order in which you compete with them.*
3. *Now put each of your top competitors (those that are either aggressively after your business or you want to get their business) on the top of a page. List everything you know about them. Also list those areas where your information is weak, inconclusive, or sparse.*
4. *Develop a strategy to discover what you don't know and effectively and professionally use what you do know.*

Keep Better Sales Records

If you don't know where you are going, it is difficult to get there. If you don't know where you have been, you are prone to repeat mistakes, errors, and failures. Effective records are a must for your success. They will drive your strengths and bring weaknesses to the surface.

1. *Create a list of every sales action you can think of: Number of telephone calls, presentations, close attempts, new prospects, number of referrals, etc. (There are at least thirty different types of information you can develop.)*

2. *Decide which of these is the most critical in your career or with your product or service.*

3. *Design a form to keep track of this information and enter information into it for two weeks.*

4. *Evaluate ratios between different types of information. For example: How many appointments do you need to make a sale?*

Develop a Closing Strategy

Closing is not just a skill. It's also an attitude. The close of the sale is a natural conclusion to everything else you have done up to that point. "I am here to do business." Most salespeople who are poor closers can trace that condition to one of either two causes: poor prospects or no closing strategy.

1. *Write out your closing sequence/strategy (winging it doesn't count).*

2. *If you don't have one, then create one.*

3. *Memorize it.*

4. *Try it out on some of your fellow salespeople, friends who are in sales, or your mother. But try it out before you use it on your best prospects.*

Evaluate Customers and Prospects

Time is money. Spending enough time with your best clients and prospects is one of the best ways to succeed in sales. Spending too much time with poor prospects and clients who can't give you much more business can be a killer.

1. *Develop a profile of information (criteria) that you can use as a template to determine whether this prospect is worth your time and resources.*
2. *Now categorize this information into A, B, and C prospects. The better the match of information in your list the higher the rating: A, B, C.*
3. *Take this template and measure each current active prospect and client against it. This will tell you whether you are spending too little or too much time with certain clients and prospects.*

Referrals

Referrals are "easier money." It is easier to do business with referrals than any other source of new prospect. Referrals can come from anywhere, but the best source tends to be current satisfied customers.

1. *Ask every customer for at least three referrals.*
2. *Develop a referral awareness. Learn to ask for referrals just as if it was ingrained in your consciousness.*
3. *Start a referral page in your binder. Every time you get one, list the source, the referral, and the result.*

Develop Better Questions

Accurate information is *the* key to your sales success. Asking good questions is a vital skill in selling. Most salespeople talk too much. They give information before they get it.

1. *Create a list of everything you need to know before you can accurately evaluate whether you have a good prospect.*

2. *Prioritize the list. Some information may be vital while other information may be insignificant.*
3. *Now develop a question to get this information.*
4. *Test the questions. If you get what you ask for, great. If not, back to the drawing board and redesign the question.*
5. *Once you have a set of questions that get you all the critical information you need to make the sale, memorize the questions.*

Tailor the Presentation

Each customer is unique. People buy according to their needs and wants, not according to yours. They buy when they are ready to buy, not when you need to sell. Avoid a feature dump. Tailor the message to the dominant emotional buying motive and to their buying style.

1. *Evaluate your selling style. Do you talk to much? Too little? Expect people to buy for your reasons? Do you project your buying prejudices into the sales process?*
2. *Get a book on behavior styles.*
3. *Develop a strategy to effectively sell to each of the four different styles.*

Letters of Testimony

Ask every customer for a written letter of testimony. Short and sweet, yet one of the most valuable exercises.

Service

Effective after-sale service is the glue in all sales relationships. It is where you deliver on promises you made on behalf of your organization. It either builds more trust and strengthens the relationship, or sabotages it when it is not present, satisfactory, or consistent.

1. *List all the ways you service (both you personally and your organization) your customer.*
2. *Call/write all of your clients and ask them to comment on your service (again, you and the organization).*
3. *Ask them how you could do a better job of after-sales service.*

Appendix 2

Resources

Audiotapes

Nightingale Conant
(800) 525-9000
www.nightingale.com

Tape Rental Library
(804) 293-3705
www.trlonline.com

Books

47 Ways to Sell Smarter
Jim Meisenheimer
Helbern Group

50 More Ways to Sell Smarter
Jim Meisenheimer
JM Associates

Advanced Selling Strategies
Brian Tracy
Fireside

Anatomy of a Successful Salesman
Arthur Mortell
Farnsworth Publishing

The Ancient Scrolls
Tim Connor
Connor Resource Group

Consultative Selling
Mack Hanan
AMACOM

The Experience Economy
B. Joseph Pine, James H.
    Gilmore, B. Joseph Pine II
Harvard Business School Press

Full Price
Thomas Winninger
Dearborn Trade

*The Greatest Salesman in
    the World*
Og Mandino
Bantam Books

Growing Your Business
Mark LeBlanc
Milt Adams

How to Sell More in Less Time
Tim Connor
Connor Resource Group

*How to Sell More in Less Time,
    With No Rejection, Using
    Common Sense*
Art Sobczak
Business by Phone
Jonathan Livingston Seagull
Richard Bach
MacMillan Publishing

Life Is Tremendous
Charles E. Jones
Executive Books

Niche Selling
William T. Brooks
McGraw-Hill Professional
    Publishing

No Bull Selling
Hank Trisler
Fell's

The Perfect Sales Presentation
Robert Shook
Bantam Books-Audio

The Platinum Rule
Anthony Allesandra
Warner Books

Please Understand Me
David Keirsy, Marilyn Bates
Prometheus Nemesis Book Co
Price Wars
Tom Winninger
St. Thomas Press
Sales Bible
Jeffery H. Gitomer
William Morrow & Co

Sales Mastery
Tim Connor
Conner Resource Group

*Sales Questions That
   Close the Sale*
Charles D. Brennan Jr.
AMACOM

Selling the Invisible
Harry Beckwith
Warner Books

Selling Leverage
William Exton Jr.
Prentice Hall

Soft Sell
Tim Connor
Sourcebooks

*Speaking Is an Audience Centered
   Sport*
Marjorie Brody
Career Skills Press/Brody
   Communications Ltd
Spin Selling
Neil Rackham
McGraw-Hill

Taking the High Road
Frank Bucaro
Frank C. Bucaro
   & Associates, Inc.

Telephone Tips That Sell
Art Sobczak
Business by Phone

Ten Greatest Salespersons
Robert Shook

Think and Grow Rich
Napoleon Hill
Fawcett Books

Magazines

Fast Company
(617) 973-0300
www.fastcompany.com
Sales and Marketing Management
(800) 821-6897
www.salesandmarketing.com

Selling Power
(800) 752-7355
www.sellingpower.com

Success Magazine
(919) 807-1100
www.successmagazine.com

Newsletters

Boardroom Reports
330 W. 42 Street
New York, NY 10036

Competitive Advantage
www.competitiveadvantage.com
e-mail: info@competitive
    advantage.com

Dartnell
(800) 621-5463
www.trainingforum.com/
    dartnell/index.html

Executive Book Summaries
(888) 358-1000
www.summary.com

Sales Strategist
(800) 266-1268
www.meisenheimer.com/nl/
Selling Advantage
(800) 220-8600
www.pbp.com/sellinga/html

Telephone Selling Report
www.smartbiz.com.sbs/pubs/
    nl18.htm

Recommended Retail Store

Successories
(800) 932-9673
www.successories.com

Recommended Sales/Motivational Speakers

Master Speakers International
www.businessbyphone.com/
    msi.htm

Recommended Seminar

American Management
    Association
(212) 586-8100
www.amanet.org/index.htm

Recommended Web Sites

Executive Books Web Site
    for Books
(20 to 90 percent discounts)
www.executivebook.com

Just Sell
www.justsell.com

Index _____

About the Author _____

Tim Connor, CSP, is a bestselling author and full-time speaker and trainer. Since 1973, he has given more than 5,000 custom presentations in 18 countries on topics such as Customer Focused Sales, Peak Performance Management, and Building Positive Business and Personal Relationships. A few of the 26 books he has authored include *The Road to Happiness Is Full of Potholes*, *The Ancient Scrolls*, and the international bestseller, *Soft Sell*. He can be contacted via e-mail at speaker@bellsouth.net or by phone at (704) 895-1230 or (800) 222-9070. Visit his Web site, www.timconnor.com.

Carla Peell

443-277-4885

(PC3) ⇒ Baltimore

Kristy   Tino

410-540-9466